CHINESE EUNUCHS

CHINESE EUNUCHS

The Structure of Intimate Politics

BY TAISUKE MITAMURA

Translated by Charles A. Pomeroy

Charles E. Tuttle Company

RUTLAND · VERMONT : TOKYO · JAPAN

Representatives

FOR CONTINENTAL EUROPE
Boxerbooks, Inc., Zurich
FOR THE BRITISH ISLES
Prentice-Hall International, Inc., London
FOR AUSTRALASIA
Paul Flesch & Co., Pty. Ltd., Melbourne
FOR CANADA
M. G. Hurtig Ltd., Edmonton

Published by the Charles E. Tuttle Company, Inc.
of Rutland, Vermont & Tokyo, Japan with editorial
offices at Suido 1-chome, 2-6, Bunkyo-ku, Tokyo

Library of Congress Catalog Card No: 77-104201
Standard Book No: 8048 0653-5

First printing, 1970

PRINTED IN JAPAN

Kangan: Sokkin Seiji no Kozo by Taisuke Mitamura
Original Japanese-language edition published
by Chuo Koron Sha Ltd., Tokyo
© 1963 by Taisuke Mitamura

Table of Contents

Table of Contents

Table of Contents

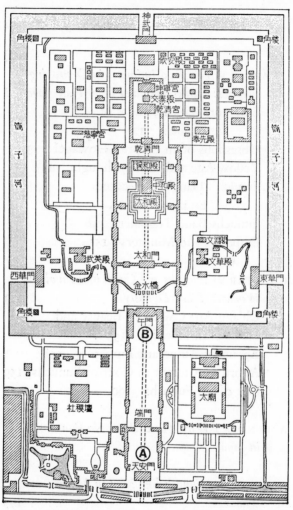

神武門

角楼　　　　　　　　　　　　　角楼

欽安殿

坤寧宮
交泰殿
乾清宮

慈寧宮　　　　　　　　　　　奉先殿

乾清門

保和殿
中和殿
太和殿

簡子河　　　　　　　　　　　　　　簡子河

文淵閣

武英殿　　太和門　　　文華殿

西華門　　　　　　　　　　　　　東華門

角楼　　　金水橋　　　　　　角楼

午門
Ⓑ

社稷壇　　端門　　　　　太廟

Ⓐ
天安門

PEKING: The inner precinct, from the T'ien An Gate [A]
through the Wu Gate [B] to Tzu Chin Palace

Publisher's Foreword

Throughout much of the long history of China, the political structure was undermined countless times by palace termites in the form of eunuchs. This is not to say that all palace eunuchs were evil. However, a system based upon greed, duplicity and thirst for power, possessing the repulsive roots of corruption, must necessarily spawn evil-doers, or at least evil followers.

One of the earliest references to Chinese eunuchs occurs in the *Tso Chuan* for the year 535 B.C., but historians generally agree that it was not until the reign of Han Huan Ti, A.D. 146–67 that this new weakness in the governmental structure became evident, destined in time to bring the empire to ruin. In fairness to the eunuchs, it should be noted that the surge in eunuch power stemmed in great part from the ambitions of the consort families and from the secluded manner of life which etiquette prescribed for the Emperor.

9

The ladies of the palace and the eunuchs who served them were in frequent and intimate association with the Emperor. The eunuchs, aware of any weakness in his character, were able to gratify his whims and play upon his prejudices. Thus the Emperor in many cases became the plaything of those pariahs from the normal world. They deftly colored for their own purposes the ruler's picture of the outside world and turned him against any ministers who tried to oppose their influence.

Under the reign of Han, the eunuchs became more powerful than the consort family had ever been.

It is easy to generalize, but extremely difficult to be objective, on a subject about which little has been recorded through the centuries. But, as the author notes in his searching analysis, it is logical to believe that the eunuchs and the unique system which embraced them, continued to wield power of varying degrees throughout the centuries.

Later centuries present more precise information on the subject and we are told with a reasonable degree of certainty that late in the sixteenth century eunuchs were recruited for the palace in groups of more than 3,000 at a time. By the end of the Ming dynasty it had been estimated that their number had grown to more than 70,000. Methods of recruitment are not clear. Self-castration was prohibited by Ming law, but men of low station and dim prospects often sought this route to influence and security. Emperors were reported to have fulminated against this practice many times throughout the dynasty, but often to no avail.

Ambitious parents who were fortunate enough to have several sons often offered one young boy for palace service. This was permitted by law, but whether these boys were castrated before or after their admittance into service is not clear.

As the number of eunuchs soared, so did the complex of agencies in which they were organized. The basic establishment consisted of twenty-four offices charged with various aspects of palace maintenance. The most prestigious of all the eunuch agencies was that of the Directorate of Ceremonial, whose director was the unchallenged chief of the palace staff. It has been estimated that the total number of eunuchs in service throughout the empire by the end of Ming, including an estimated 70,000 at the Capital, may have exceeded 100,000.

Palace eunuchs played a major role in the friction between the outer court and the inner court, and in intragovernmental strife in general. Earlier dynasties had fallen partly because of their failure to restrict eunuch access to political power, and the Ming rulers were certainly well aware of this. But they failed to prevent what turned out to be the most notorious examples of eunuch abuses in all Chinese history.

Four famous eunuch dictators arose in succession: Wang Chen in the 1440's, Wang Chih in the 1470's, Liu Chin in the early 1500's, and finally the most notorious of all, Wei Chung-hsien in the 1620's. The regular palace administration was reported totally disrupted under them.

Ming emperors relied upon eunuchs chiefly for the same reason that English kings in the fourteenth and early fifteenth centuries relied upon celibate clerics to manage their household agencies, such as the Exchequer and the Chancery. Eunuch subservience, consequently, was the most total of all, and emperors seemed to have considered them particularly trustworthy.

Shen-tsung (1572–1620) allowed twenty-five years to pass without once having an audience with his capitol administrators. Imperial decisions, ironically, were transmitted to the Grand Secretariat on papers carried by eunuchs shuttling and slinking in and out of the remote recesses of the palace. Sometimes they were even conveyed orally. Thus, improper eunuch influence in state affairs was almost unavoidable. The procedural arrangements and the organizational structure of the Ming government, except during the reigns of especially diligent and conscientious emperors, did not permit political success to any but the power-seeking unprincipled.

As in the Han dynasty, the consequence of eunuch control was unrest, turmoil, and revolt in the provinces. The fall of the eunuch Liu Chin in 1510 revealed the extent of the corruption which was honeycombing the empire. This eunuch had the enormous sum of 251,583,600 gold and silver taels; two suits of armor in solid gold, 24 pounds of unmounted precious stones, 3,000 gold rings and brooches, 500 gold plates, 4,062 gem-studded belts, and a mansion in Peking. This vast and dazzling wealth had been acquired during his service in the palace and at public expense!

But, as Prof. Mitamura says, the new and modern age finally penetrated the old world of the eunuchs, and in 1912, when the Ch'ing dynasty collapsed as a result of the republican revolution, the eunuch system died along with the autocracy that had supported it.

The wonder is that the unsavory system survived as long as it did. And the fact that the complete abolition of the system was first demanded only after the advent of the twentieth century shows how deeply the system was rooted in Chinese history.

Prof. Mitamura's original work in the Japanese met with such wide and enthusiastic response that the publisher is proud to offer this adapted and condensed English version to the general public.

Foreword

Though eunuchs played a major role in the history of Asia, particularly in China, surprisingly few books or essays have been written about these men who were deprived of their masculinity. Several reasons could no doubt be given to account for this, but it is perhaps partly due to the feeling of disgust evoked by the word "eunuch."

The first Japanese to take up the subject of Chinese eunuchs was, as far as I was able to determine, Dr. Jitsuzo Kuwabara. One of Japan's foremost scholars of Oriental history, he wrote an essay entitled "Chinese Eunuchs" that appeared in the *Mainichi* newspapers in 1923. Brought up and educated in the Meiji era (1868–1912), a time when Japan was seeking to modernize herself along Western lines, Dr. Kuwabara is thought to have written his essay with the aim of ridding Japan of her long-standing enamoration of Chinese civilization, which, as the mother culture, strongly influenced the formation of Japanese civilization. In addition to his essay on eunuchs, he also published such works as *The History of Chinese Footbinding* and *Chinese Cannibalism* as well as tracts on odd Chinese customs. These customs he denounced as being barbaric, and he congratulated the Chinese for abolishing them at the time of the 1912 revolution. He also expressed his gratitude to those Japanese rulers who had had the good sense not to import the eunuch system into Japan.

The abolition of the eunuch system in China is impressively described by Dr. Tokio Hashikawa in his "Memorandum on Eunuchs" (1959). This took place on November 5, 1924, when Hsuan T'ung Ti, the last emperor of the Ch'ing dynasty, was driven out of the Tzu Chin Palace, where he had been allowed to live after the 1912 revolution, by a *coup d'état* led by Gen. Feng Yu Hsiang. Dr. Hashikawa wrote: "Shortly after noon on that day I saw a host of eunuchs with boxes and sacks containing their belongings slung either on their backs or on sticks carried by two men. They were coming out of the Hsuan Wu Gate on the north side of the Tzu Chin Palace, crying pitifully in high-pitched, feminine voices." Dr. Hashikawa witnessed this with wonder, for he was seeing the end of a system that had endured well over 2,000 years and through twenty-five dynasties. It was reported that the number of eunuchs who left the palace at the time numbered 470.

When we think that this event took place the year following Dr. Kuwabara's essay, the realization that eunuchs, whom we are apt to view as grotesque creatures of the past, actually existed in the twentieth century is vividly brought home. For thirteen years after the republican revolution in China, eunuchs were still in existence there.

Eunuchs were not peculiar only to China. Looking back through history, we find that they existed in Egypt, Greece, Rome, and Turkey, and that they were found all the way across the Asiatic continent from the Mediterranean coast in the west to Korea in the east. In Korea, they were used much the same as in China, a practice that continued down to the end of the Yi dynasty

(1392–1910). Perhaps we Japanese were fortunate not to have had eunuchs in our past, as Dr. Kuwabara pointed out in his essay. So let us turn to China where, as already pointed out, the existence of eunuchs was of great historical significance.

The eunuchs in China, as indicated by historians in the Ch'ing period, played a fundamental part in every dynasty and its fall. Such great empires as the Han, T'ang, and Ming in particular were led directly into decline by the eunuchs, who were considered part of the political establishment. Political figures in China were traditionally classified according to two types, the "clear stream" and the "muddy stream," and it was usual to place the eunuchs at the head of the latter category because of their nature. Strangely enough, however, few Chinese scholars called for an end to the use of eunuchs, and most of them believed that eunuchs were a necessary evil whose power had only to be controlled. Although this attitude seems somewhat illogical, we can at least attain a full appreciation from it of how deeply rooted in Chinese culture the eunuchs were.

18

It is difficult to grasp the actual nature of this situation because books on Chinese history generally omit specific information on the subject. Discussions of eunuchs center around the times when their activities reached high points or when politics appear to have been distorted by them. They seldom go beyond a fragmentary presentation of factual developments. But we cannot ignore the importance of forming a thorough and consistent view of these men who lived in the shadows of China's history, for the eunuchs were active both in and behind the scenes during more than 3,000 years of autocratic rule in that country. Thus, it can be said with certainty that a study of eunuchs is an important subject in the overall study of Chinese history and not merely a result of morbid curiosity.

The present volume explains something of what eunuchs were and of the things they were concerned with. It describes their activities during the Han, T'ang, and Ming periods, with the major characteristics of these periods given in way of background.

Among the studies of eunuchs by Japanese

which I referred to in writing this book were the following, for which I wish to express my greatest appreciation.

Hashikawa, Tokio: "Kangan Oboegaki" [Memorandum on Eunuchs]. *Bungei Shunju,* December 1959.

Kuwabara, Jitsuzo: "Shina no Kangan" [Chinese Eunuchs]. *Toyoshi Setsuen*

Nishimura, Hideo: "Kodaijin no Seiteki Chishiki" [The Ancients' Knowledge of Sex]. *Gakugei,* No. 5, Vol. 5.

Shimizu, Taiji: "Jikyū Kangan no Kenkyū" [A Study of Voluntary Eunuchs]. *Shigaku-zasshi,* No. 43.

Stent, G.C.: "Essay."

Chapter I

The Artificial Third Sex

Incomprehensible Beings

In Imperial China, the term *huan kuan* was used in two senses. It meant simply a castrated man in the one sense, while in the other it meant one who served in the Imperial Palace. Other Chinese words used to indicate the first meaning were *ching shen* (purified body) and *wu ming pai* (one without official rank). The Western equivalent for these words would be "eunuch," which was derived from Greek and appears in the Bible with the same meaning. In Matthew 19, for example, it says: "For there are eunuchs who have been so from birth, and there are eunuchs who have been made eunuchs by men, and there are eunuchs who have made themselves eunuchs for the sake of the kingdom of heaven." Of particular interest to us in this biblical passage is the statement that there were men who voluntarily gave up their masculinity as an act of devotion to God. In China, voluntary emasculation of this kind was known as *tzu kung*. But even though the Chinese term indicates the same act as that committed by devoted Christians, it was actually quite different in intent. The *ching shen,* as these voluntary eunuchs were known in China, proceeded along the path, not to heaven but, in many cases, to the lower regions.

On another point, if Christ did not find it necessary to reject eunuchs, then it would appear that he found them acceptable. This brings to mind a remark by G. C. Stent, the eminent British scholar who made a study of eunuchs, to the effect that eunuchs, who were found so extensively throughout the various countries of the East, were not common in Europe because of the influence of Christianity. Stent may have been right, since eunuchs were used by the Greeks and Romans in pre-Christian Europe and then disappeared for the most part after the advent of Christianity, but the words of Christ give us a slightly different impression.

In Italy, the practice of making boy sopranos by castration for Catholic choirs was common. This was banned in the latter half of the nineteenth century by Pope Leo XIII, but the practice was continued outside the Church in order to supply such boys for operatic and theatrical groups in various parts of Europe. According to church records, there were also instances in which men, of their own volition, rid themselves of sexual desire as an obstruction to salvation, and these practices perhaps occurred because Christ did not repudiate eunuchs. A similar voluntary action took place in China, as mentioned above, but for different reasons.

The story is told about a talented and intelligent man who lived during the Ming dynasty. Since sexual desire interfered with his studies, he had himself transformed into a eunuch, whereupon he gradually lost his eyebrows and beard and became feminine in appearance. When he passed the *k'e chu,* an extremely difficult examination for governmental service, a great fuss was made over him by the other eunuchs who until then had had to suffer humiliation due to their ignorance.

23

Now they felt that they had found an intellectual champion.

Although there may have been some logic in cutting off the source of sexual desire because of devotion to God, it is difficult to understand a man undergoing castration to pass an examination, especially since the examination was considered to be the gateway to honor and riches, the prerequisites in historical China for having several wives and thus a large number of descendants. But for the realistic Chinese, the high civil position may have seemed the gateway to heaven on earth.

Whether in the East or West, those who had themselves castrated because of religious or academic reasons are called eunuchs, but they should be distinguished from the more ordinary type of eunuchs. In the West, where the word eunuch in its original Greek sense meant "bed guard," eunuchs had special tasks. So, too, did the eunuchs who served in the Chinese court. The Bible contains many references to the activities of eunuchs—who are also referred to as "officers" or "chamberlains," just as they were in China—

who ranked high in both military and civil services. These men were entrusted with special duties which enabled them to grasp and hold powerful positions.

Unlike the Greeks, the Chinese had an explanation for the existence of the court eunuchs, which was given with an air of great importance: there are four "eunuch" stars located in the astronomical map to the west of the Emperor's constellation. The idea of four eunuch stars, although thought by some to have been derived from the number of women intimately connected with the Emperor, indicated that eunuchs already had roles as attendants to the Emperor in the heavenly world. The Chinese firmly believed that the heavenly order of things applied to all humans and was behind all happenings. Thus they were able to accept the eunuch system as a matter of destiny or divine order.

Two terms for eunuchs, *an jen* and *ssu jen,* which appear in the *Chou Li,* a book of law and manners published during the Chou dynasty, throw some light on the duties of these men. An *an jen* is described as a person used to guard the

Imperial Palace, while a *ssu jen* is described as one who took care of the Emperor's mistresses and the punishment of court ladies. Whether called eunuchs or *huan kuan,* castrated men in both East and West were used as palace attendants, particularly in the women's quarters.

Origin of Eunuchs

Exactly when this practice started is not known with certainty, but some historians believe that Semiramis, the beautiful Assyrian queen who founded New Babylonia, was responsible for starting the system. Eunuchism probably did occur about the same time that the ancient Oriental autocracies were established. It is interesting to note that the historical activities of eunuchs in both East and West began to be recorded about the same time—during the eighth century B.C. Herodotus, the father of historians, said the use of eunuchs was a Persian custom and that the Persians thought such men were far more dependable than ordinary people. He also praised the Persian eunuchs for their loyalty. That eunuchs were known and widely used is borne out by the fact that the Greeks performed the emasculations and sold the eunuchs commercially. Herodotus wrote that the Greeks sold their eunuchs in Ephesus, an ancient city in Asia Minor, and Sardis, the capital of Lydia, at high prices. Sardis, it seems, was particularly famous as a market place for eunuchs.

In China around the same time, the period called "Spring and Autumn," eunuchs were employed by local lords and were active politically. They reportedly had already resorted to evil, murdering rulers and driving a prince to death with slander. Their activities prior to the eighth century B.C., when the seat of Chou rule was moved east and the "Spring and Autumn" period began, is obscure. It is thought that eunuchs existed as early as the beginning of the Chou dynasty because they are mentioned in the *Chou Li,* but the belief has not been confirmed.

However, a remarkable discovery in the history of eunuchs was made at an ancient Yin-dynasty site, where bones inscribed with pictographs were found. Dr. Shizuka Shirakawa, an authority on pictographs, exhibited a piece of bone with the two-element pictograph 𐂍 and the character for the Ch'iang people. The pictograph expresses what it was intended to convey, with the 𐂍 element meaning a penis and the 𐂍 element meaning to cut off. The Ch'iang, ancestors of the present-day Tibetans, were a race living to the west of the Yin, and the piece of bone was used by the ruler of the Yin, Wu Ting, when he consulted the gods on whether to make a eunuch of a Ch'iang.

It is clear from this discovery that eunuchs existed in China at least 1,300 years before Christ, for that was when Wu Ting reigned. The origin of eunuchs probably goes back even earlier than Yin, and there is little doubt that eunuchs existed during the later Chou dynasty.

Methods of Castration

Several methods of castration were used in ancient times. In ancient Egypt the operation was carried out by a priest, who first bound up all the generative organs with a strong strand of woolen yarn. Ashes and hot oil were used to stop the bleeding and a metal rod was inserted into the urethra. The patient was then buried in hot sand up to the navel and left that way for five or six days. The death rate resulting from such rough handling was as high as sixty percent, it was recorded.

A similar method was used in southern India, but the technique was a little more sophisticated. The subject was first seated on a ceramic chair and given opium. Then his generative parts were clamped between two pieces of bamboo and severed by sliding a razor along the wood, after which the wound was washed with hot seed-oil and covered with an oil-soaked cloth. The patient was left in a horizontal position on his back and nourished with milk until the wound healed. Very few casualties were reported.

For information on similar operations in China, we have the valuable data gathered by Stent who carried out his research during the 1870's and 1880's. According to this data, there was a little hut, called a *ch'ang tzu,* just outside the western gate of the Tzu Chin Palace where the operations were performed. Several government-approved but unsalaried specialists, called *tao tzu chiang,* worked there and made their living by producing eunuchs. The fee for the operation was six taels (about $84) and the specialist remained responsible for his patient until he was completely healed. Since most of the clients were quite poor and could not pay immediately, they would make an arrangement with the specialist to pay for their operations out of future salaries. In all cases, however, the specialists required that the clients have guarantors. Several apprentices worked under the specialist to learn the techniques, thus the profession became traditional.

In preparing for the operation, the abdomen and upper thighs of the patient were tightly bound with white strings or bandages. After the parts to be cut off were washed three times in hot pepper-water, the patient was seated in a semi-reclining position on a heated, couchlike affair known as a *k'ang* and his waist and legs were held firmly by the assistants. The specialist, with a small, slightly curved blade in his hand, then faced the prospective eunuch and confirmed his intention by asking *Hou huei pu hou huei?* (Will you regret it or not?). If the man showed the slightest uncertainty, the operation was not performed. If the man gave his consent, the knife flashed and a new eunuch was made. Both the scrotum and the penis were cut off and either solder or a plug was inserted into the urethra, after which the wound was covered with paper that had been soaked in cold water and carefully bound up. Assistants would then walk the eunuch around the room for two or three hours before allowing him to lie down.

The new eunuch was not permitted to drink water for three days after the operation and he suffered from extreme thirst as well as from his wound. The plug was removed after three days, and if urine gushed out, they knew that the operation had been a success and congratulations were exchanged. But if no urine appeared, no one could save the man from an agonizing death. However, this method of operating was so successful that Stent in his years of studying old records found only one unsuccessful case, in which a man aged thirty died.

Usually the wounds healed in about 100 days, after which the new eunuch would go to the Imperial household to learn his duties. At the end of the first year the eunuch would be transferred to the Imperial Palace to begin his new occupation.

Stent gives a most unusual account of how the severed parts were disposed of after the operation. Known as *pao,* or "treasure," the parts were processed by a specialist, put into a container with a capacity of about three cups, sealed, and then placed on a high shelf. This was called *kao sheng,* or "high position," and it is said to have been symbolical of the original owner attaining a high position. If, however, the natural owner or one of his relatives asked for its return, the *pao* was given back. In this case, too, the same care would be taken, with the *pao* being placed in a high place and prayers offered for the eunuch's advance in the world.

There were two reasons for the careful preservation of the *pao.* First, the eunuchs had to show their *pao* upon being advanced in rank, and advancement would be impossible without it. The examination, known as *yen pao,* or "treasure examination," was made by the head eunuch. The custom resulted in great profit for the specialists who performed the operations. The right of ownership lay, of course, with the man on whom the operation was performed, but at the time of the surgery some forgot to ask for their *pao.* This was seen as relinquishing the right of ownership and the *pao* became the property of the specialist, unless the eunuch later returned for it. Even the *pao* of a stranger would do, and they would pay as much as fifty taels (about $700) for one. There were also instances in which eunuchs lost or were robbed of their *pao,* in which case they would buy one from the specialist, borrow one from a friend, or even rent one.

The second reason for preserving the *pao* was so that it could be buried with the eunuch after his death. In this case, too, it was permissible to use a substitute. The eunuchs hoped to be restored to masculinity in the next world, for the Chinese had a great fear of deformity. Also, it was be-

lieved that Jun Wang, the king of the under-
world, would turn those without their *pao* into
female asses.

The above description applied to eunuchs of
the Ch'ing dynasty, but the same procedures
were doubtlessly practiced from the time of the
Ming dynasty. However, there is little information about castration in Chinese literary sources.
The only account of this sort that I have been
able to find appears in the *Chiou T'ang Shu,* a
historical chronicle of the T'ang period. It contains a story about the famous An Lu Shan who
fomented a major revolt against Emperor Hsuan
Tsung, and how he made a eunuch of one of his
servants.

According to the story, Li Chu Erh, a sly,
hard-to-manage boy of twelve or thirteen, from
the Mongolian Ch'i Tan tribe, was in the service
of An Lu Shan. One day An Lu Shan wielded
his sword and castrated the boy, who bled pro-
fusely and lay in a half-dead condition, but he
was treated with hot ashes, and recovered. Made
his eunuch by An Lu Shan, the boy became from
that time the favored and inseparable companion

of his master. Although the method of castration was barbaric, it did not differ much in principle from the other methods.

The method used by An Lu Shan was probably the same as that used in ancient times. When a man voluntarily had himself emasculated and paid for the operation, a certain amount of care was given to him. But castration was a form of punishment as well as a fate that often awaited prisoners from enemy tribes. Because of the high mortality rate, however, the practice of complete castration is said to have gradually been given up in favor of a less severe operation.

After castration, physical changes appeared in the eunuchs; they took on an unnatural, passive nature that must have made them appear monsters to normal persons. Still, in the mysterious tangle of human relations in the Imperial household, they played important roles.

Sometimes, however, a eunuch failed to lose his masculine nature even though his body was changed, and this could result in dire consequences.

Appearance and Characteristics

Although the word eunuch is not new, few of us understand its full meaning. Without a specific picture of their strange appearance and habits, it is difficult to understand their activities and the resulting influence on the historical process. Fortunately we have the report of Stent to help us learn something of the facts, but he saw only the eunuchs of the latter part of the Ch'ing dynasty. The following is based on his report.

The eunuchs dressed in a long, gray garment called a *p'ao tzu,* over which they wore a short, dark-blue coat called a *kua tzu* and a pair of black trousers. Added to this dark, somber costume was a cap. When they walked, they bent over slightly and took short, mincing steps, characteristics that made them easily recognizable even at a distance. Eunuchs were generally repulsive in physical appearance, but if they happened to be handsome and young their feminine ways made them appear like women dressed as men. As they grew older, however, they acquired an ageless, sexless appearance.

There was a distinction between those who were deprived of their sex in childhood and those who gave it up in their manhood. The latter were called *ching* or *cheng,* both words meaning "pure of body," and the former were called *t'ung cheng,* which meant "pure from birth." Favored by the court ladies, the *t'ung cheng* had no work assigned to them and behaved like young girls. Stent hesitates to say what their actual roles were in regard to the ladies, and this is left to the reader's imagination. They were replaced, of course, by younger ones when they grew older.

All the eunuchs underwent a change of voice after castration, and this was particularly true of those who were castrated in childhood. Their voices could hardly be distinguished from those of girls. After they grew up, their voices became a falsetto of very unpleasant sound. Stent compared it to the shrieking call of a woman vendor in a London fish market. Chinese actors, when playing the roles of eunuchs attending emperors and empresses, speak in artificial, half-crying voices and groan like men in pain.

Beardlessness was another characteristic of the eunuchs. The Chinese were never a people to praise a heavily bearded man, but the eunuchs almost without exception lost their beards entirely.

Another result of castration in the younger eunuchs was that they wet their beds; this was overlooked at first, but severe punishment ensued if it continued. Bed-wetting led to the description of any unbearable smell as being "stinky as a *lao kung* [eunuch]." In fact, the Chinese said that a eunuch could be detected by his smell 300 meters away.

Young eunuchs also fleshed out and became soft and fat. They had little strength, of course; as they grew older, however, many lost weight, and deep wrinkles appeared.

Character changes also took place along with the physical transformation. Eunuchs would quickly shed tears over small things or become angry over minor matters. They were seldom cruel, and usually were gentle and conciliatory. They were warmhearted, and many kept puppies as pets.

As a whole, the eunuchs tended to be strongly united, helping each other and standing together against the world. This feeling, abetted by their often influential positions, was sometimes so strong that it resulted in intense political activity. In the latter part of the Han dynasty, for example, one of the leading eunuchs discovered a plot by Grand Marshal Ho Chin, a relative of the Imperial family on the maternal side, to annihilate the entire eunuch force. Confronting the Grand Marshal with his discovery, the eunuch asked, "So you wish to exterminate our race?" and slew him with his sword. This was an example of their group consciousness as a "race" and their strong opposition to oppression by outsiders.

But this strength was effective only within their own limited environment, the Imperial court, where they had the power of their master behind them as well as their own tight bonds of fellowship. Outside the court, the eunuchs were about as helpless as babies. The leader of the eunuchs who had killed Ho Chin took the infant Emperor with him and fled during the night after a *coup d'état,* but when he was threatened with a sword by a low-ranking civil clerk he became frightened and cowardly. Bowing to the little Emperor, he said, "Your Majesty's servant is to die. May your Majesty keep well!" and threw himself into the river.

The eunuchs were extremely sensitive about their condition, and any reference either directly or indirectly to their "deficiency" insulted them. One did not, therefore, speak directly of a "tailless or bob-tailed dog" but used an euphemism such as "the dog with a deer's tail." Broken objects, such as a teapot with a broken handle, were not mentioned in the presence of a eunuch, for to call attention to it would suggest "deficiency." The Chinese also avoided using the word *ke,* which means "cut," in the presence of a eunuch because of its connection with castration.

A habit acquired by the eunuchs after the Ch'in dynasty was opium smoking. It seems that all were addicts and frequented several dens near the palace. But their greatest pleasure seems to have been gambling, at which they spent much of their time. "Life is nothing without gambling" was their motto.

The eunuchs' good points should also be mentioned: many were exceptionally honest, and kind-hearted and benevolent toward those in need. Among the merchants who regularly visited the palace, they were quite popular, for they did not attempt to beat down prices as the ordinary Chinese people did. These merchants and craftsmen kept this well in mind and would say, "Oh, at your mercy!" when meeting the eunuchs, who would pay generously even for slipshod work, often not bothering to receive their change. This increased their popularity as customers.

It is also interesting to note that, since they were considered "deficient men," a large degree of freedom was allowed the eunuchs in their speech and manners. Remarks or actions that would bring stinging rebukes to ordinary persons were overlooked in the case of a eunuch because he was "just a eunuch."

These descriptions follow chiefly those given in Stent's report. The chief characteristics of the Ch'ing dynasty eunuchs are listed, but it should be remembered that differences did exist between eunuchs at various times throughout history. A few eunuchs, because of strong personalities, played prominent historical roles and their distinction cannot be judged by ordinary standards.

When examining their strange existence, they were found to be generally neither masculine nor feminine, adult or juvenile, good or bad. The results were lamentable. When people such as these were brought into daily contact with merciless autocrats, it was only natural that peculiar relationships should develop.

Chapter II

Provenance of Eunuchs

Strong Jealousies

Why were such odd creatures needed in China? Dr. Kuwabara says they were necessary because the Chinese were inclined toward strong jealousies, which he describes as follows: "The Chinese have always been a very jealous people. This is easily understood from reading such books as the *Li Chi,* the Confucian scriptures, where rules of etiquette and manners are sensitively arranged so that there would be no imaginable chance of one being suspected of having illicit relations with the opposite sex. Under such circumstances, it may have been a matter of course for eunuchs to have been used as a means of avoiding the suspicion of immorality and soothing jealous minds in the Chinese society."

Dr. Kuwabara's opinion appears sound, but there were other reasons for a eunuch system. When the Empress Tse T'ien Wu became ruler in the T'ang dynasty, she had as a lover an energetic apostate priest who was spending most of his time in the harem. An official proposed to the throne that if the man were to be allowed to stay in the harem he should be castrated "in order to protect the chastity and purity of the ladies-in-waiting and other court ladies." The Empress, it was said, had a good laugh over this recommendation. Actually, this well-muscled priest was an acknowledged bedroom expert recommended to the Empress by a princess who had already enjoyed him, and he had had the honor of receiving the Empress' favor as well.

The necessity for eunuchs in China's polygamous society should be considered also from other points of view. Leaving this matter to be discussed later, I can say that Dr. Kuwabara's opinion is valid only after the morality of Confucianism had fully permeated the society and that there had to be other reasons for eunuchs before the "Spring and Autumn" period, the period of the "Warring States," and even further back into the Chou and Yin dynasties.

The colorful overtones of the ancient Oriental monarchies were retained down through the generations, so it is a great help in our study of eunuchs to look back to the old oracle bones for clues. In the state of Yin, a so-called theocracy, ritual observances and politics were combined. The monarchy had been established against this holy background with its king as the divine agent. Accordingly, the king turned the men of Ch'iang into eunuchs as a result of divine revelation. The Ch'iang were also sacrificial victims at the ceremony presenting prisoners of war to God. This was apparently the Yin way of expressing thanks for their victory and of asking for further victories.

By severing the symbol of manhood from their prisoners of war, the Yin no doubt sought to make the men of the conquered tribes completely subservient. This was far more effective than what was called "making a man boneless." During the reign of Emperor Wu in the Earlier Han dynasty, a young prince of Lou Lan, one of the walled states on the western boundary made famous in Inoue's *Lou Lan,* was taken hostage and made into a eunuch. Following the death of the king of Lou Lan in A.D. 92, the people of the country requested that the prince be returned to take the throne. The rulers of Han rejected the request, however, for it would have been most embarrassing if the prince's countrymen found him to be a eunuch. While showing the inconsideration of the Han Emperor, it was also clear evidence of Wu's desire for complete conquest.

Symbols of Conquest

Castration was a symbol of conquest as well as a method of revenge. Herodotus gives an example in the vendetta between Periander and Corcyrans, who had shown him much brutality. Periander, the tyrant of Corinth in ancient Greece, seized the son of a peer in Corcyra (the present Corfu in the Ionian Islands), one of the subject cities, and sent him to Sardis to be castrated.

Thus it is clear that one of the chief reasons for making men into eunuchs was the prestige it gave conquerors. It was a combination of brutality and religion that characterized the ancients. However, there was a strict rule against castrating one of their own.

Of what use were castrated captives in court? Consider the prince of Lou Lan. In spite of his noble birth, he could not return to his homeland because of his shameful deformity, nor could he enter foreign society. He was relegated to speechless solitude, cut off from almost every bond of human relationship. This loneliness resulted in what might be called a "cattle man." In China, where ideas were expressed through ideographs, punishment by castration was appropriately expressed by characters meaning "to put him down in the silk-worm room." The comparison was to the silk worms that lay like dead bodies in dark, tightly closed rooms where the temperature was kept high and the air smelled of death. Thus the eunuchs lived in a kind of subterranean world.

The forlorn condition and peculiar nature of the eunuchs made them of inestimable value to the monarchs. The monarchs were regarded as agents of God, and the original God-man relationship of ruler and ruled applied. A clear line separated the monarchs and the people. Neither God nor the monarch was to reveal what he actually was to the people—the secret door between the two worlds was always shut. But the monarch was only a man, so he led his private life behind doors in mysterious ways. He could not allow a commoner to enter his private quarters even as a servant, for that would have meant disclosing himself to his people as a mere man, and he would have lost his control over the people. Further, many treasures including beautiful women and divine articles taken from the original owners by divine right were kept in the palace. These, too, could not be touched by commoners. Since ordinary commoners could not serve in the inner recesses of the palace, who could? None were more suitable than the eunuchs, the "cattle men."

Thus the eunuch system was instituted in the name of divinity, allowing the monarch to enjoy his earthly privileges. It was quite natural then that there should be four eunuch stars placed west of the Emperor's constellation in the heavenly order of things.

This system was not exclusively Chinese. Similar situations existed in countries to the west, especially in the Islamic courts. Herodotus pointed out that the eunuchs helped maintain the mysterious distance which the king kept between himself and his subjects.

In Turkey two groups of eunuchs, one Negro and one white, guarded the harems. The head of the white group was called the supervisor of the gate, and even ministers could not gain entry to the palace without his permission. The Negro eunuchs were given more important positions than the whites and their leader was called the chief of servants. Officially he was called the "Head of the Blessed Chamber," the highest official position in Turkey, and he was the receptionist at the Sultan's mosque. The appointment of a Negro eunuch to the high position rather than a white was based on the belief that the more uncivilized the servants, the more loyalty they would show to their masters. These examples indicate how important the roles and positions of eunuchs were in religious states.

Needless to say, the characters of the eunuchs changed at various times through the centuries so that they would be in tune with the monarch's desires, but their fundamental duty of preventing confidential matters from being revealed remained unchanged as long as the Oriental autocracies continued.

Emperors' Shadows

It is evident that the relationship between a monarch and a eunuch was very much like that of a man and his shadow. Separation was impossible, but it was always the eunuch who was labeled as evil while the monarch was regarded as blameless. This viewpoint may have arisen because historians usually wrote only about the sinful activities of the eunuchs.

When Ho Chin conceived a plan for the total extermination of the eunuchs, Ts'ao Ts'ao of Wei, the famous character in the story *San Kuo*

Chih (Chronicle of Three Kingdoms), jeered at the plan and said: "The office of the eunuchs has existed as a necessity since ancient times to the present. It is the lords who are responsible for having brought the situation to such an extremity by giving so much power and favor to them. If their sins are to be punished, the root of their sins should be removed, and this could be done by a single jailer." Ts'ao Ts'ao boldly pointed out that the evil stemmed from the throne itself.

But he still stressed the necessity for eunuchs even when their despotism was overwhelming. At that time Ts'ao Ts'ao was only the head of one of the Imperial Guard units, which were under eunuch leadership. His views might be better understood if we realize that both the Emperor and the eunuch shared an extraordinary existence.

The founders of dynasties were men changed from a human to an inhuman nature. Kao Tsu of Han killed a great number of people, numbering in the hundreds of thousands. Through his able generals he was able to come to power, then he had them killed. Huang Tsung Hsi, in the *Ming I Tai Fang Lu,* criticized the later emperors for considering the country as an enormous estate, and described Chung, the younger brother of the Han Emperor, as being even more ruthless. This killer was, moreover, regarded as a great hero.

Most of the emperors were dictators. They looked with suspicion on others, and any who appeared as a threat were exiled or killed, along with their family and relatives. Ruthlessness and solitude were indispensable elements in the lives of the rulers. Thus we can see that the inhuman characteristics of the eunuchs fitted well with those of their masters.

Sources of Supply

How many eunuchs were kept in the palace? We know that in the mighty Mogul Empire of Islam, the only empire comparable to that of China in the sixteenth century, there were several thousand eunuchs. According to Dr. Kuwabara's estimate, the number of eunuchs in China ranged from around 3,000 to 13,000, depending upon the era. Although the figures vary considerably, there

were far fewer in the Ch'ing than in the later
Ming dynasty. Stent said that at least 3,000 were
required for the operation of the court. Chinese
records from the end of the Ming dynasty show
that there were about 9,000 court ladies and over
100,000 eunuchs—many of whom were said to
be starving to death. This is a surprising figure;
it could undoubtedly be called the largest empire
of eunuchs in the world.

The sources of supply underwent great changes
just as the dynasties themselves did. To avoid
intrigues and keep court secrets, eunuchs were as
a rule drawn from outside tribes or races. This
procedure remained unchanged down through
history. An example of its application is seen in
the life of the well-known eunuch Kao Li Shih,
who played an important part in history with the
beautiful Yang Kuei Fei during the rule of Emperor Hsuan Tsung in the T'ang dynasty. From
the Man Liao tribe of southern Kwantung Province, Kao Li Shih was sent to the palace by the
local military commander. Because of his shrewd-
ness he was favored by Empress Tse T'ien Wu
and attained a high position.

During the Yuan dynasty, when relations with Korea were friendly because the Empress was from that country, many eunuchs were requisitioned from Kao Li on the Korean Peninsula. P'u Pu Hua became the most powerful among this group. During the Ming dynasty, Emperor Yung Le, a man of eccentric tastes, acquired a princess from the Tungusic Nu Chen tribe, so there were a large number of eunuchs drawn from the Nu Chen people. In the reign of Ying Tsung it is said that 1,565 boys from the Miao people in Kuei Province were castrated, but that 329 died of disease and thus an additional number were required. Also, when Yunan was subjugated a large number of the conquered were made into eunuchs. This, however, was the result of an arbitrary decision on the part of the local commander and the eunuch overseer, and when the Emperor later learned of it he was displeased.

They had done it, they said, to exterminate the tribe and thus prevent future rebellions. It was a terrible deed, but the culprits went unpunished because the supply of eunuchs was necessary.

Also, some of the generals were secretly putting eunuchs in their own service.

Castration as Punishment

A second source of eunuch supply was provided by the form of punishment known as *kung hsing,* or castration. This was, in fact, one of the main sources of supply. One of the five ancient means of punishment mentioned in the *Shu Ching,* which included tattooing, cutting off the nose, cutting off the feet, execution, and castration, *kung hsing* literally meant "imperial punishment" and was applied to both men and women, using different means of course. *Kung* indicated the genitive organ. Another term for this kind of punishment was *yin hsing,* but it was usually used when the punishment was carried out because of illicit relations.

The meaning of "illicit relations" is a bit different from that of illicit intercourse and referred to the relationship between a man and a woman who were not married. A formal marriage, known as *liou li,* required procedures involving a matchmaker, an exchange of betrothal presents, and a ceremony. In the feudalistic system of the Chou dynasty, with its king, lords, and military men, all members of the ruling classes had to follow the procedure. Failure to do so resulted in what was called "illicit relations." A formal ritual of this kind was not required among the common people, whose weddings were completed with the single expression *yeh he,* which meant simply "intercourse in the fields." Men were punished for "illicit relations" by castration, but evidently women were merely locked in the palace for the duration of their lives. The punishment of women, in comparison with that of men, would seem to have been much more lenient. Some Chinese scholars were of the opinion that the punishment took the form of the severance of some part of the reproductive organ or else a sharp blow to the abdomen in order to damage it.

Castration was second only to execution in the order of severity among the punishments. It is believed to have had its origin early in the Chou period for the purpose of keeping the feudal society orderly. With the exception of execution, the five punishments were said to have been abolished by the wise and kindly Emperor Wen, but the *Shih Chi* (Historical Chronicles) say that only three were abolished.

Scholars also disagree concerning an order by the succeeding ruler, Emperor Ching. He issued an edict that allowed prisoners sentenced to death to choose castration instead, called in this case *fu hsing,* but meaning the same thing as *kung hsing.* The disagreement centers on whether the term *fu hsing* was derived from the putrid smell of the wound or from the belief that if the man were castrated he would be like a rotten tree, unable to bear fruit.

However, the next strong ruler, Emperor Wu, was responsible for the castration of such noble and brilliant men as Ssu Ma Ch'ien, who is called the father of Chinese history; Li Yen Nien, a musical genius of the era; and Chang He, whose father and younger brother were high officials in the Yu Shih Tai Fu, an important political office. Emperor Wu also had the prince of Lou Lan made into a eunuch.

Emperor Kuang Wu, who established the Later Han dynasty after the brief interlude of rebel rule that followed the Earlier Han, commuted all death sentences to castration. Successive emperors followed this precedent and even extended the use of castration to punishment for treason and other political crimes. Castration as a punishment was abolished outwardly in the Sui dynasty, but it did not really die out. During the Ming dynasty the enlightened ruler, Hsuan Tsung, frequently had military stewards castrated. Commoners, too, such as forty salt laborers who were castrated, were not free from the threat. But the trend was away from this source of eunuch supply.

Changes in Supply

A big change in the eunuch source of supply occurred during the T'ang dynasty. Until T'ang, eunuchs were with few exceptions obtained from conquered tribes or races. But during that dynasty local officials were ordered to offer to the palace men who had already been castrated. It was the responsibility of the officials and the burden of the common people. All the necessities of the court, including eunuchs, were regarded as offerings to the Emperor, and they came from all parts of the country. This was not regarded as inhuman in T'ang, for the social structure was classified by law into the noble, the commoner, the peasant, and the slave classes.

In response to this new condition, the provinces of Fu Chien (Fukien), Kuang Tung (Kwantung), and Kuang Hsi (Kwansi), in the southern part of the country, became the chief centers for the supply of eunuchs, for a number of reasons. Southern China, during the T'ang dynasty, differed from the heartland in that it was under a special administration resembling colonial rule. Consequently, conditions and attitudes were not the same, and whereas traffic in human beings was prohibited in the heartland, it flourished in the south. This practice is said to have had its beginning after the southern natives, the Man Chung and the Liao Chung, were conquered and some sold. Slave traders became more and more active in the area from that time on until even the Chinese themselves became part of the trade. These places became in time the main sources of slaves for the heartland.

Kuang Tung (also Kwantung or Canton), an important center for sea trade, was often visited by the vigorous Arabian merchants. As traders from Islamic countries, where the necessity for eunuchs was no less than in China, the Arabs were interested in extending their contacts to various countries for the acquisition of black and yellow eunuchs. Chinese slavers were doubtlessly sailing out on their own in search of slaves.

Later, during the reign of Tai Tsu in the Ming dynasty, the private castration of children by influential or rich men was banned. In issuing the ban, the word *huo chen,* which was derived from an Indian word, was used to refer to castration. The use of a foreign word, and its incorporation into the Chinese language, gives some indication of the degree to which eunuchs were imported into China.

It was clear that in addition to the activities of the Moslems and the demands of the T'ang, secret slave trading had turned the Kuang Tung area into the main eunuch market. This finally resulted, toward the end of the T'ang dynasty, in a small eunuch empire in southern China that was established by a trader. His descendants trusted the eunuchs. The last king entrusted the entire administration to his eunuchs, while he dallied with the female attendants or the Arabian ladies in the seraglio. It is truly astonishing to think that for the good of the kingdom all the competent ministers and indispensable officials were castrated—including some who had themselves emasculated before entering government service. At one time there were as many as 20,000 eunuchs in this small kingdom. The development of such a system was partly due to the sadistic interest and profligate disposition of the rulers. Although there were many eunuchs in southern China, the area probably is more significant in the history of China for its policy of promoting eunuchs.

The sole example of a eunuch from Ling Nan

who achieved much fame was Kao Li Shih. However, eunuchs from Fukien Province, another big center of supply, gained control of the political situation in the T'ang dynasty and made their names known in all parts of the country. Further, they firmly maintained this tradition from the end of T'ang down to the Ming dynasty. There is a story that once during the T'ang dynasty a local official, upon assignment to a new post, visited the grave of a late eunuch from Fukien. Other high-ranking eunuchs from the same province appreciated this rare gesture and recommended him as a district official. As a result, people gave him the nickname Ch'ih Shih Mu Hu, meaning, roughly "Keeper of the Eunuch's Grave by Imperial Appointment."

Another reason why Fukien became a center of eunuch supply was its geographical location. A mountainous area with little arable land, it was relatively unproductive and could not support its population, which naturally fell prey to the slave dealers. An incident illustrates the situation: a kindly government official asked one of his handmaids about her family, only to hear that her nine sisters had all been sold to officials as slaves and that her old mother led a lonely life at home. In sympathy, the official burned her contract and set her free. Even today there are many Chinese living in the South Seas and other areas who had to migrate from Fukien and Kwangung because the land could not support them.

To become a eunuch and to advance in the world as a eunuch were quite different matters. Unlike the bureaucrats, it was not necessary to have a high education or administrative ability. The ideal eunuch was young, dandyish, elegant in manner, and clear and sweet of voice. He had to be shrewd. The eunuch should be viewed as leading the life of a man-actress in the lascivious atmosphere of the seraglio of the T'ang. Apart from appearance, however, the manner of a man-actress was not easily acquired. One of the reasons why eunuchs from Fukien became distinguished is that they possessed outstanding traits.

Yet another reason can be given: Fukien was

known as the home of perverted sex relations between men.

Perversion in China is said to have had its beginning during the Six Dynasties period and to have been the cause of many divorces when the practice was most prevalent. In Fukien this unusual custom became popular on a wide scale and was ardently practiced irrespective of age. The older perverts were called *chi'i hsung* and the younger ones called *ch'i ti,* resembling somewhat the Japanese *chigo* and his companion. When a *ch'i hsung* went to the home of a *ch'i ti* he was welcomed by the whole family as if he were a bridegroom. If the *ch'i ti* were later to marry, the *ch'i hsung* would pay all the expenses. There was even a special word, *chi,* in Fukien that was used when a *ch'i ti* had illicit relations with another man. And if a one-sided love affair developed, the disappointed lover would sometimes commit suicide.

According to some Chinese scholars, the perverse relations common in Fukien originated with the piracy that was also practiced by men from that area. It was believed that if women were taken aboard the ships, the ships would be cursed and overturned by the sea god. So men were used instead of women.

Although the recruitment of eunuchs was compulsory in the T'ang period, it was not a punishment. Even the poor who had been degraded to the status of slaves in the strict class system could by a strange twist of fortune be ranked with the ruler and reign.

Excess of Eunuchs

Castration by one's own volition was not a form of punishment, but was based upon the economic principle of supply and demand.

Ssu Ma Ch'ien's *Shih Chi* says that castration by one's own volition was of ancient origin. Ssu Ma Ch'ien also found the following incident worth recording: When, during the "Spring and Autumn" period, the famous Ch'i asked the bed-ridden Kuan Chung whether Shu Tiao should be chosen as his successor, Chung replied that because Tiao had had himself castrated in order to be next to the Emperor, an action that was against humanity, he was not to be trusted. We can look upon Tiao as the pioneer of the type.

During the Warring States, the Ch'in and Han periods that followed the "Spring and Autumn" period, there were no recorded cases of castration by self-volition. This does not mean there were none; toward the end of the Later Han dynasty, there seems to have been a large number of self-castrated men. The method was officially recognized in the tenth century, during the early Sung dynasty.

The official recognition of self-castration took the following form in the Sung dynasty. An applicant had to first present himself to the military authorities. A day was then selected and the castration carried out, with the military authorities recording the event. After the wound had healed, the new eunuch was sent to the palace. If he were appointed to office, his day of castration would be marked as his birthday, for it was then that his second life began.

Seemingly contradictory limitations, however, were imposed. Tai Tsu in the Sung dynasty limited the number of eunuchs in the palace to fifty and banned the trading of castrated children because he had learned a lesson from untoward acts of eunuchs in the T'ang dynasty. The policy was aimed chiefly at reducing the injurious effect of having too many eunuchs. Successive rulers in the Sung dynasty followed the precedent, so that the undesirable effect of the eunuch system was far less than in the T'ang period. However, when the romantic era of Huei Tsung arrived, the traitorous type that included T'ang Kuan and Liang Shih Ch'eng again became manifest. Under the guise of recovering lost territory, they persuaded the Emperor to go to war, thus destroying the country.

It should be emphasized, however, that the official recognition of self-castration gave the period a new significance. From the historical point of view, great changes took place during the transition from the T'ang to the Sung dynasty, with the social class system of T'ang abolished and more personal liberty allowed the people. Social position was determined by one's possessions, and a spirit of enterprise and utilitarianism was awakened. A cultured man had only to pass the state examination in order to attain high position. Some among the lower classes, lacking the means to reach high position through the examination system, chose another road to influence—eunuchism.

This trend became stronger in the Ming era, leading one Emperor to conclude that anyone having himself castrated was only aiming at rank and wealth. The appetite for food and sex are among man's strongest, but how was sexual desire to be satisfied when a man had to struggle against the continual threat of starvation? Countless men went through life without enough money to get married. What was manhood worth to such men? To many it was only a shadow, a shadow that could be sold to the devil in return for good fortune and sometimes high position.

This evil system reached its climax in the Ming dynasty, leading the ruler to prohibit self-castration for the first time. It was a historical precedent. The Ming dynasty had been ushered in by the return of administrative power to the Men of

Han, the Chinese, after hard centuries under the Mongols, and the empire was in high spirits, strengthened by greater emphasis on the morality of Confucianism. One of the principles of Confucian morality was filial piety and the continuation of the family line. In the textbook of filial piety, the *Hsiao Ching,* it was clearly stated that filial piety began with taking care of the physical body received from one's parents, but the eunuchs automatically lost their source of filial piety. Consequently, the Ming administrative code, the *Huei Tien,* called for capital punishment for those who had themselves castrated because it was against the tenets of filial piety and treasonous. Individuals, village heads, and even clans were punished if they concealed knowledge of such acts.

What was the result of this prohibition? A look at the *Huang Ming Shih Lu,* a compilation of facts by the government on voluntary castrations that occurred during the Cheng Te era of mid-Ming, gives some idea. It describes the eunuchs as pulling the strings behind the Emperor and gaining privileges for themselves and their families, and then says that the lower classes, upon seeing this, competed by having their children or grand-children castrated out of a desire for wealth and rank. It reported that in one small village alone the number castrated reached the hundreds despite the strict prohibition.

A look at authentic records shows that, while voluntary castration was prohibited, eunuchs were still accepted by the palace. Government officials even made allowances for voluntary castration, resorting to such subterfuges as claiming it was caused by a riding accident or a childhood disease.

The *Jih Chih Lu*, a scholarly work written by Ku Yen Wu at the end of the Ming and the beginning of the Ch'ing dynasties, states:

"From the time of the Ching T'ai era of Ming, some people desired to become eunuchs by having themselves castrated. For a while these people were punished by the Imperial Court, but in the end they were accepted and taken into service. As a result, people living near the capital who feared being drafted into the government's compulsory labor force or who dreamed of wealth and rank were continually imitating these eunuchs and having themselves or their descendants castrated, and thronged to the military headquarters where eunuchs were managed. From that time their number increased day by day and month by month into hundreds and thousands, until they finally brought colossal harm to the country."

Major Social Problem

This was a major social problem of the times, embarrassing the government, for only a limited number of eunuchs could be employed. During the third year of T'ien Ch'i at the end of the Ming dynasty there were 3,000 vacancies and 20,000 applicants.

What were these poor men to do? During the Cheng Te era about 3,500 of these failures presented a joint petition to the government asking to be taken in. The government designated Nan Yuan, a vast park with orchards and ponds, in the suburbs of Peking, as a place for them to stay.

71

The number of eunuchs admitted into the park increased by tens of thousands, and an enormous sum was expended on rations.

The government finally sent them back to the provinces. But since the eunuchs had no place to go, they became homeless wanderers in the southern part of Hopei Province. Many became beggars or highway robbers. Local officials ignored them, with the result that they preyed upon the ordinary people.

According to Stent, seventy to eighty percent of the eunuchs of this period were castrated during childhood because of the poverty of their parents. He says that those who became eunuchs voluntarily after the age of twenty did so out of admiration for the wealth and position of high-ranking eunuchs. Many were lazy, Stent says, and cites the following cases:

The first concerns a man who had been married for two or three years, but became so stirred by the desire to become a eunuch that he could not eat or sleep. His relatives refused to be his guarantor, a requirement by the surgeon specialists before they would operate. Finally, he castrated himself. But he still did not obtain a position and eventually committed suicide.

Another case concerned a eunuch serving in a government office. He had castrated himself with a butcher's cleaver and then found employment in the Wang Fu office five years before Stent became acquainted with him. The eunuch would occasionally return home to visit his wife and daughter. When asked why he became a eunuch, he replied that it was the result of seeing his rich friends and his desire for a pleasant life for himself, his wife, and daughter.

The third case, which happened in 1853, astonished even Stent. A poor man attempted to pawn his coat. When the pawnbroker refused to take it, the man became angry, pulled out a sharp knife, and emasculated himself, throwing the parts on the counter and demanding thirty chao. The startled shopkeeper reported the incident to the authorities, who sent the man to a temple for treatment and later gave him a job in the Wang Fu office.

Chapter III

Residents of the Women's Quarters

One Hundred and Twenty-two Wives

In prewar China, sprawling mansions could be seen in the elite residential sections of Peking. Inside those mansions the world-famous Chinese concubine system continued to flourish even after the Republic was formed.

Ku Yen Wu, in arguing against the evils of the eunuch system, pointed out that eunuchs acquired power because there were too many concubines in the Imperial seraglio. He further said that it was necessary to remove the source of carnal pleasure if the ruler were to be freed from the influence of the eunuchs. This opinion was indeed revolutionary. Ku Yen Wu was an advocate of celibacy who left his wife at home and wandered through the land with three carts of books.

According to the Chinese, all systems instituted by the ancients must be observed, and the system in question was certainly one of these. The *Shih Chi* has it that the dawn of Chinese history began with the "Five Emperors" (Wu Ti) and that the first Emperor was the "Yellow Emperor" (Huang Ti). The *T'ung Tien,* a work by a T'ang prime minister called Tu Yu, says that during the rule of the son of the Yellow Emperor, Ti K'u, four queens were introduced to surround the Imperial Throne after the fashion of the four legendary "queen stars." The brightest of these stars was called the "true" queen and the remaining three were referred to as "secondary" queens. It is thought that the four "eunuch" stars, mentioned earlier, corresponded to the four queen stars.

The emperors of China seem to have been destined to have four queens in accordance with an immutable law of nature (Islam also teaches that a man may have four wives). Four was considered a sacred number that symbolized the four cardinal points. By including the Emperor, the number came to five, and "five" was also sacred. Both numbers were thought to have mystical significance and to symbolize the entire universe, so that by taking four queens, each of whom represented a cardinal point, the Emperor could regard the whole world as his domain. Thus, as Heaven's proxy on earth, the Emperor had no choice but to have four queens. In Japan, however, monogamy has been the rule largely because of the legendary descent of the Japanese from the two deities, Izanagi and Izanami, and partly because of Western influence.

One exception to the rule was the saintly Chinese Emperor Shun, who dispensed with the "true" queen because he had already taken a wife while still a peasant and had not reported this to Heaven. The system was not changed until the Hsia dynasty, which followed the period of the "Five Emperors." Since Emperor Shun took only three queens and since three times three equals nine, it was argued, the Emperor should have a total of twelve queens. According to the Chinese, the numbers "three" and "nine" are mystical and denote the ultimate limit of numbers in general. Furthermore, multiplication was thought to denote an unbreakable union, which in this case probably referred to the relationship between man and woman. By multiplying three by three, which is supposedly pregnant with infinity, one gets nine, which means "infinity."

The Chinese hoped that the magic of these numbers would bring them an infinite number of progeny. A citizen of the Han dynasty said in 30 B.C., "If you marry nine women at one time, you have more children. This is the same as respecting your ancestors."

Using a strange system of calculation, the number of Imperial concubines was increased even further in the Yin dynasty, when it was argued that twenty-seven more concubines should be added to the twelve because three times nine equals twenty-seven. This brought the total to thirty-nine. The popular belief that things spreading out in a fanlike fashion are auspicious no doubt strengthened the case. Thus, there were three groups of three added in the Hsia dynasty and then three groups of nine added in the Yin dynasty.

But the real reason for these increases was more pragmatic. The citizen of Han quoted above also said that men usually remain potent at fifty, while women lose much of their appeal at age forty. To this way of thinking, there is no age limit for men where sex is concerned, but women reach the age of retirement at around forty.

In the Chou dynasty, the number of women around the throne totaled 120, with three groups of 27 (a total of 81) added to the increase of three groups of 9 (a total of 27) previously mentioned. Also, the "true" queen dispensed with by Emperor Shun was reinstated in the Chou dynasty, following the precedent set by Emperor Ti K'u. In the *Chou Li,* said to have been written by the saintly Chou Kung, the Imperial concubines are listed according to rank, with "one *hou,* three *fu jen,* nine *chin pin,* 27 *ku fu,* and 81 *nu ju.*"

The Imperial concubine system as described above was probably not historically factual. Presumably, it was worked out by scholars of the Han dynasty who specialized in etiquette and protocol. Still, we should not pass over it lightly, for in the T'ang dynasty it was officially recognized and, accordingly, 100 Imperial concubines did exist, though under different designations.

Like Huang Tsung Hsi, Ku Yen Wu advocated a reduction in the number of eunuchs, branding the *Chou Li* and its argument for the necessity of Imperial concubines as an infamous work that taught the emperors nothing but debauchery. He did not hesitate to criticize even the sacred tomes of Confucianism. By abolishing all Imperial concubines with the exception of the Empress and the three lesser consorts, as Ti K'u did, he claimed that the number of eunuchs could be reduced to only a score or more. These two authorities were vociferous in their criticisms of the eunuch system, yet never once did they call for its abolishment.

What was the actual situation in regard to the Empress and the concubines? An example from the Han dynasty will give some idea. A learned man in the Earlier Han made the following report to the Emperor, Yuan Ti: "The Emperors Kao Tsu, Wen, and Kei had only ten or so court ladies, but Emperor Wu, however, acquired several thousand beautiful women for his harem, which was filled to capacity as a result. This custom soon became both widespread and excessive. The

79

feudal lords, for instance, acquired as many as several hundred concubines, and wealthy officials and citizens kept as many as a score or more of singing girls. This led, on the one hand, to more and more wives being forced to sleep alone, and on the other, to an increase in the number of bachelors because of the shortage of women."

During subsequent dynasties, the number of concubines seems to have increased steadily. It is said that several thousand concubines vied with one another for the Emperor's affections during the reign of Emperor Hsuan Tsung in the T'ang dynasty. One source has it that the number of concubines totaled an unprecedented 40,000, if the concubines of both Ch'ang An and Lo Yang are included. Understandably, the problem of who should share the Emperor's bed proved to be a difficult one. One solution was for the competitors to play a backgammonlike game, with the winner gaining the right to spend the night with the Emperor. Notwithstanding, Emperor Hsuan Tsung claimed the consort of his son, Shou Wang, because he was unable to find a woman to please him among his innumerable concubines. The consort was Yang Kuei Fei, a great beauty.

Since the concubine system of the T'ang dynasty served as a precedent for subsequent dynasties, it should be explained in greater detail. Included were the Empress, the 4 consorts (Kuei Fei, Shu Fei, Te Fei, Hsien Fei), the 9 ladies under the Empress, the 9 *Chou P'in,* the 9 *Chieh Fu,* the 9 literate ladies, the 27 *Pao Lin,* the 27 *Yu Nu,* and the 27 *Ts'ai Nu*—a total of 122. The addition of Kuei Fei, who in formal ranking was placed immediately below the Empress, accounts for the increase in the T'ang dynasty.

"One-set" Marriage System

Historically the Chinese tend to regard all human affairs as divine revelations, and this also applied to matrimony. The poet Tu Fu, in his *T'ung Tien,* begins with the sentence: "In the beginning, there were one man [Ti K'u] and four women [the Empress and the three lesser consorts]." This view in regard to matrimony has continued among the Chinese for thousands of years. "The matrimonial system," a Chinese has said, "is the same as a tea set. Who in the world would think of having only one teacup for one teapot?"

This viewpoint may be the reason why the Chinese have produced so few poems or stories of passionate love. Being realists, they presumably established the "one-set" system, which calls for only one role for one woman, because they believed it impractical for one woman to assume the duties of wife, lover, mother, dry-nurse and maid. The more women, the richer the content of life—for the men, that is. Such a system, of course, required money and power for a man to support more than one wife, so it was adopted by only a small segment of Chinese society, including the Emperor at the top. Even dependants of wealthy families were able to keep concubines. But the lower classes, the masses, practiced monogamy.

If jealousy involved the monopoly of one's mate, then it would seem to have applied more to women than to men in the Chinese system. Lin

Yutang, the noted Chinese author, made a wise comment in this regard: "It is easy to understand that women grew increasingly jealous with the institution of the concubine system. After all, jealousy was the only weapon with which a woman could defend herself. Through sheer instinct, a jealous wife was able to keep her mate from accumulating concubines."

Scholars of the Ming dynasty were tireless in writing about the evils of jealous women. In the *Wu Tsa Tsu,* a collection of essays rich in anecdotes, the author, Hsieh Chao Chi, says: "Confucius says that women and men of small character are difficult to manage. As a rule, women possess such undesirable qualities as jealousy, stinginess, obduracy, sloth, inaptitude, foolishness, cruelty, short temper, suspicion, gullibility, attachment to trivia, displeasure, worship of heretical religions, and infatuation. Of these, jealousy is the worst. Therefore, a woman who is not jealous makes up for a hundred faults." He follows this by saying: "The wit and intelligence of women are hardly worth mentioning. It is said that women should place feminine charm above

83

everything else. This is indeed a wise saying."

Another anecdote recalled that at a certain gathering, a frustrated husband defended his overly jealous wife, in somewhat paradoxical terms, saying: "The carnal desire of men of intelligence and noble character knows no bounds. Therefore, one can cultivate patience by marrying an unmanageable woman and by being tied down by her. Is it not said in the adage 'One finally realizes the merits of a jealous wife upon reaching old age?' "

Hsieh Chao Chi also says in the *Wu Tsa Tsu*: "As a rule, jealousy tends to increase with a woman's station in life. And strange to say, jealous women seem to live longer. Those who have to put up with such women for a lifetime are certainly ill-starred." He continued, saying that long ago a general who could no longer stand his wife's jealousy hired an assassin to get rid of her. The assassin, however, got no further than wounding her ten fingers. Three more attempts were made on her life, all of them abortive. The general, therefore, had no choice but to spend the rest of his life with her. Emperor

Ming of the Sung dynasty found a way to deal with jealousy. He had the jealous wife of one of his subjects caned twenty times, granted the husband a concubine, and made the wife live apart. For jealousy of a more serious nature, Emperor Tai Tsu's method is to be recommended. The Emperor of the Ming dynasty had the wife of Ch'ang Yu Ch'un, a famous general, executed and pickled her body in salt, then distributed it among his subjects.

If the jealousy of Chinese women was indeed so great, and if the men could do little about it, what then could the Imperial seraglio, in which several thousand desperate concubines vied with one another, have been like? The mere thought staggers the imagination. If jealousy was a woman's last resort against the "one-set" matrimonial system, men had no alternative but to take countermeasures. One such step concerned the duties of woman as expounded by Confucianism.

In Confucianism, fidelity, obedience, and sincerity were emphasized as the three cardinal virtues of a woman. Accordingly, very strict rules were laid down. For instance, when a married woman visited her parents, she was not only forbidden to sit with her brothers but also forbidden to partake of the same food. It is interesting to note that this precept was supported by Pan Chao, the younger sister of Pan Ku, who helped her brother complete his famous tome, *Han Shu*. She lauded the three ways of obedience and the four duties of a woman in her work *Nu Chieh*. The three ways of obedience refers to the fact that a woman should obey her parents before marriage, her husband after marriage, and her eldest son after her husband's death. In Pan Chao's case, it is hard to tell whether she was a traitor to her sex.

The duties of a woman were first expounded in the Han dynasty, at the same time Confucianism was proclaimed a state religion. Before that time, little thought was given to fidelity on the part of women.

The strategy for curbing the jealousy of women seems to have produced satisfactory results in the Later Han dynasty. Emperor Shun of Later Han had four concubines of the *Kuei jen* rank whom he regarded with equal affection. Since he could not make up his mind as to which should be Empress, he had them draw lots. His ministers, however, pointed out the rashness of such an act and proposed that the Emperor follow certain standards in selecting his Empress. They advised that the family background should be taken into consideration; next, the candidates should be judged as to virtue; if they were equally virtuous, age should be the next consideration; and if they were of the same age, appearance should be the final quality judged. After much consideration, Liang Shang's daughter was chosen for the final interview. She passed the test with a masterful show of verbal ingenuity. She said that the Emperor would be granted a large number of descendants and a hundred happinesses if his Empress was not of a jealous nature. It is ironical, however, that this eventually brought about the arbitrary leadership of the Liang family, leading to the downfall of the Later Han dynasty.

Judging from these circumstances, it is not difficult to understand why only eunuchs could handle the affairs of the Imperial seraglio, which might be likened to a garden of thorny flowers.

Rise of Fearsome Wives

China underwent a major change between the end of the T'ang dynasty and the beginning of the Sung dynasty. Sovereigns, officials, and eunuchs alike changed greatly in character. This transformation eventually led to a confrontation between the bureaucrats and the eunuchs, the two major political groups, in the Ming dynasty.

These changes were also evident in the relations between men and women. The rise of "fearsome" wives, for instance, is a case in point. And the bureaucrats, who were supposed to constitute a rival force opposed to the eunuchs, were actually at the mercy of their foe, especially during the Ming dynasty.

According to scholars of the Ming dynasty, fearsome wives first appeared on the Chinese scene in the tenth century. To illustrate, Chu Ch'uan Chung, who killed the last Emperor of the T'ang dynasty and later established the Later Liang, the first dynasty in the Five Dynasties period, was powerless before his wife, Chang Shih. This one-time bandit who dealt in illegal salt was reported to have hurried to his wife whenever she called, no matter where he happened to be. Again, Li K'e Yung, a Turk who became the first Emperor of the Later T'ang dynasty, reportedly respected his wife Liu Shih to the extent that he discussed all vital issues of war and state with her. These two, then, were probably China's first henpecked husbands.

In what way did relations between the sexes change after the tenth century? To begin with, neo-Confucianism was expounded in the Sung dynasty. The basic tenets of this new philosophy were racial solidarity in the face of national danger, and the preservation of racial purity. The people were urged to create healthy homes and raise as many children as possible. Keeping up the family line then became a categorical imperative in the name of filial piety. And all this touched the core of maternal instinct.

From the Sung dynasty onward, women concentrated on being good wives and wise mothers; they remained confined in their homes and raised no objection to their husbands keeping concubines. When Nanking was in grave danger as a result of the major offensive launched by the invading Chin Army, Shi K'e Fa, the mainstay of the Nanking régime, was urged by his child-less wife to take a concubine and have her bear his child.

Another anecdote bears out the far-reaching influence of neo-Confucianism. Beleaguered by the Chin army, a city in Kwangtung Province ran out of provisions. It was decided, therefore, that the soldiers defending the fortress should partake of the inhabitants, beginning with the aged. When it came time for an old woman to die, her daughter-in-law offered to take her place. She was duly boiled and eaten—and highly praised for her virtuous deed. Again, a wife offered to die in place of her husband. She said, "We still do not have any children. If he is killed now, the family line will surely come to an end."

The neo-Confucianists lost no opportunity in spreading the new doctrine, which included such customs as *ch'an chu,* or foot binding. Girls' feet were tightly bound with cloth and encased in small shoes, so that the feet never grew larger than those of a small child.

In the Five Dynasties period, Emperor Li Yu, of the Southern T'ang dynasty, who was known as a sensual poet, is said to have originated the custom by having the feet of one of his beautiful concubines tightly bound with silk and then having her dance on a gold lotus pedestal embellished with rare gems. Thus, dwarfed feet came to be euphemistically called *chin lian* (golden lotus) or *juei lian* (auspicious lotus) and the custom was widely practiced by Chinese women until the establishment of the Republic.

Lin Yutang points out that dwarfed feet had a carnal significance. Men, he says, were attracted by the strangely appealing sight of tottering women, and women, accordingly, adopted the custom in order to seduce men. Lin concludes that dwarfed feet may well be called the ultimate deception produced by the sexual fancy of the Chinese.

Why did the neo-Confucianists encourage such a restrictive custom? The answer is simple: walking was no easy matter for women with dwarfed feet. It was such an ordeal that women preferred to stay home, which resulted in less contact between the sexes. Women serving in the Imperial court were required to remove their bindings because of the danger of falling.

The great Confucianist Chu Tzu was extremely active in spreading the custom in Southern Fukien, not only to cultivate the virtues of the Chinese people but also to keep the sexes apart. As a result, it came to be regarded as a symbol of confinement and oppression of Chinese women.

The roll-back tactics of the neo-Confucianists, however, were countered by a wholly unexpected source—children.

Chi Chi Kuang, of the Ming dynasty, was a brilliant general and strategist of great fame, but he was also a henpecked husband—because of his son.

One day on the battlefield, he was forced to execute his son, according to military law. On hearing this, his wife forbade him to keep concubines. But the general secretly kept a concubine who bore him two children. His wife heard of this and wrathfully declared she would get rid of both the concubine and the children. The general summoned his wife's younger brother, who was also his subordinate, and said, "The best way is to keep the children and give up the mother. If the children are killed, I vow to take my men and first kill your sister, then you, and finally your entire family. After that I will surrender my office and title and leave for good. I will let you know that I am there by beating a drum in front of the gate. Now, hurry to your sister."

The brother visited his sister and begged her to do as the general wished, but she rejected the first two alternatives. In the meantime, the general beat his drum outside. Weeping, the brother said, "If you are killed, that cannot be helped. But I cannot bear having the whole family killed." This was too much for even his strong-willed sister. She agreed to take care of the two children on condition that the concubine be caned thoroughly and sent away. Several years later, the general's wife died and the concubine returned. The general was widely praised for his brilliant strategy. He had succeeded not only in keeping the family line intact but also in passing on to his children the hereditary office he acquired through his military achievements.

Contemporary scholars of the Ming dynasty claimed that husbands who had achieved fame in officialdom became henpecked since they feared that rumors from inside the walls of the Imperial court would harm them. Men of intelligence, therefore, were beset with worries in upholding the family name; further, they had to look after their concubines who numbered a score or more.

"The master of a household must be both foolish and deaf if he hopes to remain one." This adage, widely quoted from the T'ang dynasty onward, eloquently describes the situation. It was coined by Emperor Tai Tsung when he was counseling Kuo Tzu I, a trusted and competent subject. The "craftiness" of the Chinese "gentleman," then, is certainly not an overnight product.

Of the many Chinese who had an eye for money, the concubine dealers of Yang Chou took full advantage of the situation and accumulated vast fortunes, for the Yang Chou concubines were in great demand during the Ming dynasty. Although Yang Chou women were rarely of extraordinary beauty, they were soft and pleasant to the touch, probably because of the excellent quality of local water. Moreover, they were strictly educated in terms of etiquette and were taught to humbly obey the formal wife at all times.

In the final analysis, most of the officials of the Ming dynasty who were victims of their wives seem to have been egocentric opportunists. "Ants gather before putrid meat, and flies are attracted by odoriferous waste. Our officials are no better."

Chapter IV

In the Palace

Duties of Eunuchs

Not too much is known about the duties performed by the eunuchs at the Imperial court. A glimpse into the Ming dynasty, however, should give a general picture, for the eunuch system was apparently firmly established during this period.

Tzu Chin Palace was the sanctum of the emperors. Generally speaking, Peking consisted of the Inner Precinct and the Outer Precinct. The Imperial Palace or the Inner Precinct occupied a rectangle about three kilometers long and two and a half wide, with a gate on each side. The gates are the famous T'ien An Gate (called Ch'eng T'ien Gate in the Ming dynasty), the Main Gate or South Gate, in front of which lies a plaza (where festivals such as National Day and

May Day are held today), the Pei An Gate on the north side; and the Tung An and Hsi An gates on the east and west sides, respectively. The common people were forbidden to enter the Palace compound during the Ming dynasty.

To the north of the main gate and beyond the Juei Gate stands the Wu Gate, the largest castle gate in the world, leading directly to Tzu Chin Palace. The Palace itself, which is one kilometer long and 760 meters wide, is surrounded by a wide moat called T'ung Tzu He. Lesser officials were not allowed to enter the Palace, even when circumstances called for them to report to the Emperor; they could go no farther then the Wu Gate. The gulf between Emperor and subject, the Chinese claim, can be likened to that between Heaven and man.

The Wu Gate leads to a magnificent array of brilliantly colored wooden structures, adorned with yellow roof tiles and built atop a white triple-tier marble platform. The central office here is the Huang Chi Tien (also called the Feng Hsien Tien), where high-ranking civil and military officials formerly gathered to celebrate New

Year's Day, the winter solstice, and the Emperor's birthday, the three major festivals, and to observe other important state functions.

Tzu Chin Palace is divided into two parts, the east side and the west side, by the Ch'ien Ch'ing Gate, which stands about 600 meters north of the Wu Gate. In the Ch'in dynasty, the area north of the Ch'ien Ch'ing Gate was referred to as the Inner Court, where the Emperor and his family lived, while the area between the Ch'ien Ch'ing Gate and the Wu Gate was called the Outer Court. All told, the Tzu Chin Palace consisted of 786 structures, including various buildings, pagodas, and gates.

Who inhabited this sprawling palace? To begin with, three or four cabinet ministers occupied the quarters situated to the east of the Wu Gate. Here, however, even the premiers were considered no more than porters.

The regular male inhabitants consisted exclusively of the Emperor, or the master of the Imperial Family, the Crown Prince, and the lesser princes. But even the princes were granted mansions and sent off to remote cities as soon as they received their kingship. This left only the Empress, the Imperial concubines, the court ladies, and the eunuchs. Since the cabinet ministers met the Emperor only on special occasions, the private and official affairs of the Emperor were handled by the eunuchs, who spent both day and night by his side. Small wonder, then, that they acquired power.

Kao Li Shih, a eunuch, called Emperor Hsuan Tsung of the T'ang dynasty Ta Chia (Honorable Master), while the Emperor in turn called him "our old servant." In the Ming dynasty, the Empress called the Emperor Hei Chai (Husband), and the eunuchs referred to the Emperor and Empress as Wan Suei Yei (Old Master) and Lao Niang Niang (Old Madam) or Niang Niang (Madam). Since these words were widely used in ordinary families, it shows that a mutual feeling of familiarity existed between the eunuchs and the Emperor and Empress. Huang Tsung Hsi's definition of eunuchs as "inner subjects" and officials as "outer subjects" is undoubtedly in deference to such deep human relations.

In the Ming dynasty, the national budget and

the Imperial budget were as a rule handled separately. During the course of a year, the Emperor spent about 1,000,000 taels from his personal silver reserve, and another 240,000 taels was spent by the Kuang Lu Ssu, or the Imperial Household Agency. The Emperor, therefore, spent about eighteen million dollars annually. Such a large sum, however, hardly covered expenses. Everything belonged to the Emperor, and the people were not only expected to pay for palace repairs and construction but also to offer various goods as gifts.

The Imperial household consumed as much as sixteen million kilograms of firewood, nine million kilograms of soft charcoal and used 28,000 silver taels' worth of carpets and curtains a year. Such extravagance was even more marked during the Wan Li era, toward the end of the Ming dynasty, when luxury was the order of the day. The Imperial concubines alone spent about 400,000 taels on cosmetics, and entertainment called for as much as two million taels. The wedding of an Imperial prince cost an incredible twenty-four million taels. The Emperor himself had to raise money, and the eunuchs were employed for this purpose.

Twenty-four Official Agencies

What precisely was the nature of the duties discharged by the innumerable eunuchs in this vast palace? Liou Juo Yu, a learned eunuch of the late Ming dynasty, gives a detailed description of court affairs in his chronicle *Chuo Chung Chih*. A study of this work shows that, in the Ming dynasty, eunuchs served in 24 official agencies, divided according to function into 12 bureaus, 4 departments, and 8 sections.

The Nei Kuan Chien bureau was in charge of all construction and civil-engineering projects throughout the nation, and also procured copper, tin, wood and iron utensils and implements to be used by the Emperor. Through its many local branches, it supervised repairs of the mansions of local kings and the mausolea of the emperors and empresses.

An Annamese eunuch who possessed a genius

for construction was reported to have made all the ponds, castle gates, and palaces in Peking. Construction and civil-engineering projects proved to be extremely lucrative undertakings for eunuchs, since such projects invariably involved graft. For example, in the first year of T'ien Ch'i, 30,000 of the 500,000 gold taels granted by the Emperor to build a mausoleum were pocketed by the eunuchs. Again, it was rumored that buildings and fixtures for the Imperial court cost several hundred times more than they should have.

The Yu Yung Chien bureau procured screens, chairs, tables, and other furniture for the Emperor. The backgammon and game boards, playing cards, mother-of-pearl work, and elaborate red lacquerware, made from such materials as ivory, Chinese quince, rosetta wood, and sandalwood, were handled by this bureau. It was another lucrative source of income for the eunuchs.

Draperies, cushions, and outfittings for the Imperial cortège for the Emperor's outings, and also summer and winter rattan blinds, raincoats, umbrellas, were made in the Ssu She Chien bureau.

The Yu Man Chien bureau looked after the Emperor's horses and elephants. Cows were kept in separate stalls and put out to grass in the pasture beyond the castle walls. The horses were kept in stables in the northern and southern parts of the capital.

The eunuchs employed in the Shen Kung Chien were in charge of cleaning the Imperial Mausoleum, burning incense, and lighting the altar candles. It was customary for the Emperor to worship at the mausoleum, situated outside the palace proper, on the first day of May, August, and November.

The Shang Shan Chien office was in charge of offering food three times a day to the Emperor's ancestors enshrined in the Feng Hsien Tien, as well as preparing court meals and banquets. The Emperor's meals were prepared, in turn, by the Ssu Li Chien, or chief eunuch, the Chang Yin Ping Pi, or chief secretary of the eunuchs, and the chief of the Tung Ch'ang, or the secret police.

Originally, the Kuang Lu Ssu, or Imperial Household Agency, served the Emperor's meals, which were often less than pleasing to his palate.

The task was transferred to the eunuchs after the Emperor found the food prepared by one of his eunuchs highly palatable.

The culinary art soared to great heights in China, for the Chinese believed that improvement of the art of living was a vital force in cultural development. Since the Imperial court never lacked money and supplies, the eunuchs were usually gourmets and culinary artists of the first order.

The Imperial seals were made in the Shang Pao Chien. Well over 30,000 seals, made of precious stones, were used in a single year. In Japan, community life may be said to begin and end with seals. This custom was borrowed from the Chinese.

In China, Imperial seals were symbolic of the Emperor himself. So great was the power represented that anyone possessing the seals of the previous dynasty was acknowledged as the rightful monarch. Seals, therefore, were not only comparable to the Three Sacred Imperial Treasures of Japan, but also formed the basis of the Chinese power structure.

Written appointments of peerage, official documents and checks were kept in the Yin Shou Chien.

Despite the impressive name, the eunuchs employed in the Chih Tien Chien merely cleaned the Huang Chi Tien and other structures in the Outer Court used for official functions. The Emperor's ceremonial robes, everyday apparel, headgear and footwear were made in the Shang I Chien. The following episode took place there:

One day, on hearing that his favorite pearl-incrusted garment was missing, Emperor Wan Li flew into a rage. The three eunuchs suspected of stealing it desperately tried to put the blame on one another. One of them died, and the remaining two succeeded in convincing the Emperor that the dead eunuch had stolen his garment. Actually, one of the Emperor's favorite court ladies had stolen it and sold it through her attendant eunuch.

When the Emperor visited the Outer Court, the eunuchs in the Tu Chih Chien swept the roads and acted as guards. They were considered the lowest class since they had to work even in severe cold.

Next in order were the four *ssu* or departments.

Hsi Hsin Ssu: Firewood and charcoal for the palace were handled here. The eunuchs of this department also dredged ditches and kept the tanks full of water for fire-fighting purposes.

Chung Ku Ssu: Clad in bright garments, the eunuchs employed here played various instruments as they led the Imperial processions when the Emperor visited the Outer Court. They also beat drums when dragon ships engaged in mock battles during the Double Five Festival. Since this department was also charged with staging theatricals, it had about 200 actors. At harvest time, for instance, the eunuchs would stage a harvest scene. Playing the parts of a peasant couple and an official, they would act out a scene where the official collected taxes from the couple, who complained about the unfairness of the burden placed upon them. This served to enlighten the Emperor on the labor and suffering of the farmers. The actors also staged shadow-picture plays, in groups of ten or more, on many occasions.

Puppet shows were performed during the summer months. The dolls, which were about fifty centimeters tall and without legs, were manipulated by eunuchs hidden by a partition across the stage. The puppet stage itself was an elaborate affair, with a built-in aquarium designed to take the edge off the summer heat. These shows usually dealt with the adventures of the heroes of such popular literary works as *San Kuo Chih* and *Hsi Yu Chi*.

Pao Ch'ao Ssu: Again the impressive name is deceptive, for the eunuchs employed here merely produced toilet paper for the eunuchs. Toilet paper for his Majesty was produced by the Nei Kuan Chien and turned over to those in charge of the Imperial lavatory. Emperor Wan Li, incidentally, used expensive toilet paper produced in Hanchow.

Hun T'ang Ssu: This is another name for the eunuchs' bathhouse, which was later abolished because an enterprising Buddhist priest set up a bath in his temple and employed as attendants a number of "volunteer" eunuchs who had failed to pass the official eunuch examinations. The new bath was such a success that all of the eunuchs immediately preferred to bathe there.

Of the eight *chu*, or sections, the following two are most worthy of note:

Ping Chang Chu: Swords, lances, suits of armor, bows and arrows, and firearms, which were referred to as sacred weapons, were produced here. The gunpowder section was a subdivision of this section. In the Ming dynasty, only eunuchs were allowed to handle firearms. Since this meant that the regular army had no firearms, the eunuchs, during wartime, took charge of this division. This is only one instance among many that shows how fully the Ming rulers trusted the eunuchs.

Wan I Chu: This was the only office situated outside the Imperial Palace. Here court ladies expelled from the palace were kept in confinement to prevent court secrets from being revealed.

The remaining sections consisted of the Yin Tsuo Chu, where silver pieces to be granted to meritorious subjects by the Emperor were made; the Chin Mao Chu, where the eunuchs' headgear was made; the Chen Kung Chu, where the summer and winter garments of the eunuchs were made; the Nei Chih Jan Chu, where wine and flour for the court ladies and eunuchs were made; and the Ssu Yuan Chu, where vegetables were raised.

Besides the twenty-four offices, eunuchs served in the innumerable Imperial warehouses, as timekeepers, and some even looked after cats.

Vast Tzu Chin Castle formed a world cut off from the common world, where the eunuchs produced whatever the Emperor required, provided him with entertainment, and discharged court duties. The eunuchs who held the highest office were the Tai Chien, or chiefs of the twelve *chien,* or bureaus. Their posts were equivalent to the fourth official grade, which ranked them immediately below the deputy ministers of the external ministries. Even those who were once slum children, ne'er-do-wells, hooligans or criminals were appointed to lofty posts. A disenchanted scholar of the Ming dynasty writes that he was amazed to learn that a fine mansion with a magnificent flower garden in which many sweepers were working was the villa of a eunuch whose sole function was to supervise carters. Small wonder, then, that "volunteer" eunuchs flocked to the palace.

This, however, does not mean that every eunuch who served at the Imperial court achieved success. A large number spent their lives as lowly laborers. Such eunuchs were called Ching Chun.

Eunuchs in Charge of Imperial Bedchambers

The familiarity that existed between the ruler and the eunuchs was of a special, intimate nature; nothing like it existed between the ruler and his "external" subjects.

As previously mentioned, An Lu Shan was extremely fond of a eunuch called Li Chu Erh. In his late years, Lu Shan grew so fat—about 195 kilograms—that his potbelly hung down to his knees. When the Emperor had his sash tied, Chu Erh supported Lu Shan's enormous paunch with his head, with attendants assisting and doing the actual tying. Again, when Lu Shan bathed in the hot spring at Ch'ing Hua Palace, it was Chu Erh who helped him disrobe. These facts show that the arch-villain, Lu Shan, put absolute faith in Chu Erh. Later, Ch'ing Hsu, Lu Shan's son, took advantage of this trust and inveigled Chu Erh into fatally stabbing Lu Shan in his enormous pot-belly.

Eunuchs participated in the nocturnal activities of the ruler. In the Ming dynasty, the office charged with the duty of looking after the Imperial bedchamber was called Ching Shih Fang, and the eunuch in charge was called the Ching Shih Fang T'ai Chien, or Chief of the Imperial Bedchamber. This office dealt exclusively with the nocturnal relations between the monarch and his consort and concubines.

When the Emperor had relations with the Empress, the date was recorded so that it would serve as proof in the case of conception. The procedure differed somewhat in the case of concubines. *Lu t'ou p'ai,* or nameplates painted green at the top, were prepared for the Emperor's favorite concubines. At dinner the eunuch in charge of the Imperial bedchamber would place as many as a score of these nameplates on a silver tray and take them to the Emperor with his meal. As soon as the Emperor finished eating, the eunuch would kneel before him, holding the silver tray high above his head, and await instructions. If the Emperor was not in the mood for love, he would dismiss the eunuch with a curt "Go." If he was interested he would pick up one of the nameplates and turn it over, face down. The eunuch would then hand the nameplate to the T'ai Chien in charge of carrying the concubines to his Majesty's bedchamber. When the time came, the T'ai Chien would strip the chosen concubine, wrap her in a feather garment, and carry her on his back to the Imperial bedchamber.

The eunuch in charge of the Imperial bedchamber and the T'ai Chien would then wait in front of the bedchamber a given length of time, at the end of which the T'ai Chien would shout, "Time is up" (*Shih shih Hou Le*). If the Emperor didn't reply, the call was repeated, and if he still did not reply after the words were repeated a third time, the eunuch would enter the bedchamber and carry off the concubine. He would only ask the Emperor if he wanted the concubine to bear his child. If the Emperor answered in the negative, the T'ai Chien would take proper contraceptive measures; if the Emperor answered in the affirmative, he would record the date so that it would later serve as proof. This was no small matter since a concubine's future position depended on whether or not she bore a child for the Emperor.

Exactly when this system was made official in the Ming dynasty is not known, but it was adopted in the Ching dynasty because, it is said, Emperor Shih Tsu believed its enforcement would keep his descendants from indulging excessively in sex. Also, the system was undoubtedly enforced in order to ensure succession in the autocratic system. Imperial life was more flexible at the Yuan Ming Yuan Detached Palace, where Emperor Ch'ien Lung was said to have stepped out frequently for a change of air.

It should be noted that, in the seraglio, the words of the Empress carried much weight. The Emperor, for instance, could not visit the chambers of his concubines whenever he felt the urge to do so. In such cases, the concubine of the Emperor's choice would first receive from the Empress a written notice to the effect that his Majesty would pay her a visit. Without the Empress' seal, the notice would not be valid, and without the notice the Emperor would be turned back.

Emperor Hsiao Tsung, the great ruler who launched the Ming restoration, did not keep any concubines. His anxious relatives and retainers urged him to keep at least twelve, as prescribed in the ancient system, in order to increase the number of his descendants. The Emperor agreed, but was never able to do so because of objections of the Empress. As a result, the Imperial Tomb contained only the Emperor and Empress, whereas the tombs of successive emperors contained their concubines as well as their consorts. "His Majesty was indeed like a hermit, the like of which we have never seen in our entire history," was the comment of a scholar of the Ming dynasty.

The eunuchs were also in charge of the Emperor's sex education. In the Ming dynasty, several Buddhist statues were enshrined in the

Inner Court. Of esoteric Lamaist origin, these strange images were in the form of men and women and beasts locked in carnal ecstasy. Buddhist, Taoist, and Lamaist halls, where eunuch Taoists and priests served, were also set up in the Imperial court. In preparation for the nuptials of the Emperor or Imperial princes, the eunuchs would have them worship these images and then, by intimately caressing the images, educate them in sexual love.

Such intimate relations between the eunuchs and the rulers were established early in childhood. As soon as he was old enough to leave his nurse's side, an Imperial prince would be instructed in speech, table manners, deportment, etiquette, and knowledge by the eunuchs. In other words, he literally grew up with them. Emperor Wu Tsung of the Ming dynasty, who was profligate in his ways, always listened to his T'ai Chien, Wang Wei, although he never lent an ear to what his retainers had to say, because he had grown up with the eunuch, sharing the same desk and studying the same books. The Emperor called him *Pan Pan,* or friend.

Influential Court Ladies

Besides the eunuchs, the court ladies had considerable influence at the Inner Court, although their activities almost always remained beneath the surface. Even the eunuchs had to join hands with them if they were to exercise their influence to the full.

Although she could hardly be called a court lady, the Emperor's nurse who fed him in his childhood occupied a vital position. The Imperial Family of ten lacked warm family ties, so the Emperor usually thought fondly of his nurse. As soon as the prince she had fostered ascended the throne, the nurse was accommodated in the seraglio, where she joined the eunuchs and wielded much power. Nurse Wang Sheng, who served Emperor An of the Later Han dynasty when he was about to lose his throne, and nurse Ke, who fostered Emperor T'ien Ch'i of the Ming dynasty, are typical cases. This practice continued unbroken from the Han dynasty onward.

In the Ming dynasty, when a Kung Chu, or

116

Imperial Princess, married a commoner, she moved to the Shih Wang Fu within the Palace compound, accompanied by an aged court lady who functioned as a steward. Such court ladies were called Kuan Chia P'o, while the commoner husbands of the Imperial princesses, who were chosen for their looks or because they were sons of the rich or the military, were called Fy Ma. They lived in the Ch'ang An mansions within the Palace compound, and visited their Imperial wives whenever they were called. In such cases, the Kuan Chia P'o proved to be major obstacles since the husbands could meet their wives only through the aged court ladies, who looked on them with contempt. On each visit, therefore, the husbands of the Imperial princesses had to present the court ladies with large sums of money. The commoner husband of Emperor Wan Li's younger sister died of frustration because the court lady assigned to his wife would not let him see her. He had not paid enough. The princess spent the rest of her life as a widow.

One day the commoner husband of Emperor Wan Li's favorite daughter visited her without going through the Kuan Chia P'o, since the latter happened to be in the midst of a drinking party with her eunuch lover. On learning of the husband's visit, the furious court lady, made bold with wine, not only turned back the husband but also responded with vile abuse to the excuses offered by the princess. Thoroughly piqued, the princess reported the court lady had earlier given her mother a slanderous account of the happening. The unhappy husband, on the other hand, was given a bloody beating at the hands of the eunuch and his friends and sent fleeing without his shoes, just as he was about to report to the Palace to present his side of the story. Furthermore, the hapless husband, accused of arrogance, was sent off to the university, where he spent three months rebuilding his character, and was denied further access to the Imperial court. The court lady was assigned to another post, but nothing was done about the eunuch.

This is in sharp contrast to the times of the Han and T'ang dynasties when the Imperial princesses enjoyed unlimited power. The court ladies of the Ming dynasty were able to act boldly only because they had the cooperation of the eunuchs. This unruly trend eventually led to an abortive attempt on the life of Emperor Shih Tsu. Although it is widely known that an emperor of the T'ang dynasty was assassinated by eunuchs, never before had an emperor's life been threatened by court ladies.

One October night, in the twenty-first year of Chia Cheng (1542), a number of court ladies suddenly attacked the sleeping Emperor. Some slipped a rope around his neck, while others stuffed his mouth with cloth or mounted his midriff in an attempt to strangle him. As he was about to die, the Empress, who heard him vomit, came to his rescue with her servants. Later in the morning, the minister in charge administered medicine, such as peach kernels, Tibetan saffron, and rhubarb pills in an attempt to draw out blood from the unconscious Emperor. It is said that his Majesty let out a groan and vomited blood about noon, and was finally able to talk in the evening.

Yang Chin Ying and fifteen other court ladies were accused of this heinous crime and, of course, executed. Nothing, however, was known of the motive behind the attack. Lady Wang, a concubine of the *ning p'in* rank, is said to have been the leader. It was also reported that Lady Ts'ao was a member of the conspiracy, since she had shared the Emperor's bed immediately before the incident. Again, it is believed that the Empress accused her because of jealousy. At any rate, the true nature of the incident was never brought to light. Nevertheless, it shows that by joining forces, the court ladies and eunuchs often had their way.

This incident led to unexpected developments. Emperor Shih Tsu was so pleased with the Way of Hung practiced by Taoist T'ao Wen Chung that he made him a full count and granted him ministerial privileges.

Hung Pills

The Way of Hung consisted of a secret formula for producing Hung pills, which were also known by a more euphemistic name (*Hsien T'ien*

Tan Ch'ion). The menstrual discharges of beautiful maidens, thirteen or fourteen years old, were gathered in gold and silver vessels and transferred to a mortar, where *wu mei shuei,* a compote of smoked half-ripe plums, was added. In such cases, maidens with coarse hair or throaty masculine voices or those who had been sick were carefully avoided. The strange concoction was then dried seven times and finally heated after adding powdered milk, cinnabar, imported pine resin, and dried and powdered human waste. The Hung pills, thus produced, were considered a powerful restorative capable of curing 5 kinds of fatigue, 7 kinds of wounds, and general debility.

Restoratives and aphrodisiacs of this nature became extremely popular in the last half of the Ming dynasty, which was marked by unprecedented cultural developments. The secret of the Hung pills was given by Taoist Wen Chung to T'an Lun, the war minister, who was widely known for his military achievements, and to Chang Chu Cheng, the powerful premier of the time. Overuse of the pills, it was reported, was responsible for the premature deaths of the two.

In the thirty-first year of Chia Cheng, Emperor Shih Tsu by Imperial edict, had 300 maidens between the ages of eight and fourteen brought to the Palace from Peking and adjacent areas, and another 106 the following year, solely for the purpose of producing Hung pills.

It can be assumed that the abortive attempt on his life, as previously described, made the Emperor an addict of these restorative pills, for the incident plunged him even deeper into Taoism. The Emperor's faith in medicine undoubtedly stemmed from his belief that he had been saved as the result of the medicine administered to him when he was on the verge of death.

At any rate, the Emperor's addiction to Hung pills had ill and far-reaching effects. For instance, Emperor Mu Tsung, his successor, became a regular user of the pills at the advice of the eunuchs and, as a result, let his genius run to waste. Emperor T'ai Ch'ang, in whom the people placed great hope, died the same night he took these pills during an illness. Later this incident, referred to as the "Hung Pills Incident," became a major political issue.

Married Eunuchs

The fact that some eunuchs, who bore the stigma of impotency, were married can rightly be considered strange, but such cases were numerous. Even the diabolic practice of castration, then, seems to have been ineffective relative to the natural instincts. It is not too difficult to understand why eunuchs, who were constantly frowned upon by the male sex and, therefore, experienced a devastating kind of loneliness, sought such unions to acquire spiritual peace.

There were also bold eunuchs who tried to regain sexual potency. Eunuch Lao Ts'ai whose name was cursed by the people of Fukien Province because he was extremely harsh in collecting taxes, illustrates this. At the advice of a necromancer, he reportedly killed virgin boys and ate their brains in a desperate attempt to reproduce his genitals. This method was apparently popular among eunuchs of high rank, for as Stent points out, arch-villain Wei Chung Hsien did the same after executing seven criminals.

The affair between Wei Chung Hsien and Kuo

Tzu, Emperor T'ien Ch'i's childhood nurse, was widely known and gave rise to all kinds of rumors. Late in the Ming dynasty, T'ang Chen, a scholar of the Yang Ming Hsueh school, discussed this incident in *Ch'ien Shu,* a work he produced to draw attention to the lamentable state of affairs in his time. He says: "Lady Ke had an affair with a T'ai Chien, Wei Ch'ao. But later, Chung Hsien, erstwhile protégé, stepped in to form a triangle. One night while the three were sipping wine before a hearth in the Ch'ien Ch'ing Palace, the two inebriated eunuchs started quarreling over their mutual lover. Awakened by their shouting, the Emperor passed judgment on the two, and Wei Ch'ao was demoted because Lady Ke sided with Chung Hsien. She defended him presumably because he was strong, whereas Chung Hsien was weak. This was confusing since it was hard to tell what she meant by strong and weak. It is recorded that some eunuchs remain sexually potent after castration, that some even grow genitals, although such organs were much smaller than normal, and also that this can be done artificially. (I dismissed such reports as nonsense, but later found that such indeed was the case.) Two concubines kept by a T'ai Chien—who served Emperor Lu Wang of Southern Ming, who had fled to Chekiang Province—asserted that their master was really capable of performing the sexual act.

As previously described, the sexual relations of the eunuchs were almost always confined to court ladies. And it is apparent that such relations existed as far back as the Han dynasty since the term *tuei shih,* which denoted the conjugal life of eunuchs and court ladies, was widely used at that time.

Court ladies who married eunuchs employed lesser eunuchs as cooks. Popular opinion of the time has it that the greater part of the inhabitants of Peking, especially women, were lazy gluttons. Such women, however, were no match for the married court ladies. Competent eunuch cooks, therefore, were in great demand among the *ts'ai hu* court ladies, some even earning as much as four or five silver taels a month.

Eunuchs who remained single after the death of their mates were praised for their virtue. A scholar who was staying at a Buddhist temple discovered that a locked room contained the memorial tablets of the departed wives of eunuchs. On death anniversaries, the scholar reports, the eunuchs would show much more grief than ordinary widowers.

Many eunuchs not only married other than court ladies, but also kept concubines. The gay district of Peking was full of houses accommodating concubines kept by such eunuchs, who were usually high-ranking officials.

Fate of Eunuchs

Acquisition of power spelled death for many eunuchs. Some were executed, while others, victims of conspiracy, were demoted to the rank of laborers and eventually killed. However, some eunuchs achieved both success and fame and lived out their lives in affluence.

Eunuchs in general came to be regarded with hatred by the public and were considered obscene. The ultimate destiny of eunuchs, however, hardly differed from that of ordinary people. Many spent insignificant lives, serving night and day at the Imperial court.

In the Ming dynasty, an An Le T'ang, or house of rest and comfort, was built for such eunuchs. Here court and lesser eunuchs received treatment when they fell sick. When a eunuch died, the eunuch in charge at the house would apply for a special copper pass and carry the dead eunuch to the Ching Le T'ang, a special crematorium for eunuchs. A coffin and firewood for cremation would be supplied by the Nei Kuan Chien and Hsi Hsin Ssu, respectively.

There was also a crematorium where the court ladies and eunuchs without kin were cremated. Eunuchs were buried apart from their families since they considered themselves akin to priests. They even referred to castration as the act of entering the priesthood.

Richer eunuchs pooled their funds and formed fraternities that went by sorrowful names so that they could be sent off in style to the other world, amid an appropriate chorus of sutra-chanting.

Chapter V

The Two Intimates in Destroying Empires: Earlier Han and Later Han

Emperors Raised in Laps of Eunuchs

After the downfall of the Ch'in Empire, the Han Empire, a world power of the first order, ruled China for four centuries and established many of the forms of Chinese culture. The first two centuries of the Han dynasty are referred to as the Earlier Han dynasty, and the second two as the Later Han dynasty. Historians theorize that the Earlier Han dynasty was toppled by the relatives of the Empress, while the Later Han dynasty was brought to ruin by the eunuchs.

The first Emperor of the Han dynasty was no doubt familiar with the troubles that attended succession and other matters. Nor is it hard to visualize the Emperor resting his head on a eunuch's lap, for with eunuchs he could feel at ease. Thus it would seem that most historians have thought too lightly of the role of eunuchs as comforters of the rulers.

This role is even more clearly illustrated in the case of Emperor Ling, the last ruler of the Later Han dynasty. Widely know for his deep attachment to eunuchs, the Emperor is said to have frequently referred to Chang Jang and Chao Chung, both Nei Ch'ang Shih chamberlains, as "Chang Jang, my father and Chao Chung, my mother." But Emperor Ling was called a foolish ruler; perhaps it was because of his foolishness that he was able to express his affection for eunuchs in candid terms.

These examples show that the monarchs of the Han dynasty, from the first to the last, not only required the presence of eunuchs but considered them the mainstay of their lives. The eunuchs constituted an indispensable power group close to the throne from the outset of the Han dynasty.

Obsessions of an Empress Dowager

The first Emperor of the Han dynasty owed the credit for many of his achievements to Empress Lu, his hardy wife.

A large number of subjects were reported executed at the instigation of the Empress because she feared that they would eventually bring disaster to the dynasty. The Emperor and Empress worked hand in hand in most matters, but when it came to the problem of succession, the two were worlds apart.

At that time, the Emperor was extremely fond of Prince Ju I, his son born to Lady Ch'i, his favorite concubine, who implored him to make their son Crown Prince. The Emperor had long been thinking of doing so, especially since the prince looked very much like him. Empress Lu, of course, had no intention of letting her son be removed as Crown Prince, and vowed revenge, even though her son retained his post.

When the Emperor died, Empress Lu poisoned Prince Ju I and vented her wrath on Lady Ch'i by gouging out her eyes, making her deaf and dumb by means of smoke and drugs and confining her in a lavatory, calling her a human pig.

Heaven, however, did not let such diabolic atrocities go unnoticed. Shocked by such cruelty, Emperor Huei bemoaned the inhumanity of the acts and took to bed. From then on, the ruler completely neglected politics and indulged in wine and sex, day in and day out. When he died several years later as the result of such debauchery, Empress Lu is said to have cried aloud without shedding a tear.

Following Huei's death, the political situation took an unexpected turn. The prince who ascended the throne was not the real son of Emperor Huei's wife. Feigning pregnancy, the childless Empress had killed the mother of the infant prince, who was a concubine, and claimed him as her own. Upon learning the truth, the young ruler declared he would some day avenge his mother's death. Empress Lu, therefore, kept him confined deep inside the palace and established herself as ruler.

If the founders of the Han dynasty had lived in a society in which the maternal system still prevailed, there would have been nothing strange about the emergence of Empress Dowager Lu.

The founders, however, introduced into the dynasty a matriarchal system peculiar to them through their revolution. This system formed the basis of the maternal power groups. Under the system, the Empress Dowager governed with the assistance of either her father or elder brother, who was appointed commander of the Imperial Guard.

It should be noted that eunuchs were indispensable to the system. In the Han dynasty, the living quarters of the Emperor and Empress Dowager were called the Wei Yang Palace and Ch'ang Le Palace, respectively. As in the Ming dynasty, men as a rule were forbidden access to the Imperial seraglio. However, some men served at the Inner Court as officials during the Earlier Han dynasty. Officials serving at Ch'ang Le Palace, however, were almost exclusively eunuchs.

Since the Empress Dowager received the ministers in audience only on important occasions, orders were passed on to them by the eunuchs.

This obviously was of advantage to the eunuchs. Sometimes the Empress Dowager would discuss vital political matters with the eunuchs; the eunuchs gradually came to participate in government and eventually acquired power.

Empress Lu's favorite eunuch wielded great power not only as Huan Che Ling, or chief eunuch, but also as the head Yeh Che, or eunuch in charge of guarding the palace gate and receiving visitors. He was the first eunuch to become a peer. This shows that eunuchs automatically acquired power as the result of the system in which the Empress Dowager became regent.

Surprisingly, under the system, the number of criminals decreased, the peasants worked harder, food and clothing became plentiful, and the land was at peace. Obviously Empress Lu was too busy with court affairs to carry out political reforms, and this was a welcome change to a peace-seeking people exhausted as the result of drastic reforms effected by the Ch'in Empire and the civil strife that followed.

Yellow Age and Moral Thought

The aged retainers of the Han dynasty who did away with the entire Lu family after Empress Lu's demise were extremely prudent in choosing the heir to the throne, obviously because they did not want another puppet ruler. Their ultimate choice was Prince Tai, or Emperor Wen, as he was later called, not only because he was calm and moderate but also because he had no influential maternal relatives.

A laissez-faire attitude, variously called "Yellow Age" and "Moral Thought," both of which refer to the pessimistic doctrine expounded by the Yellow Emperor and Lao-tze, was favored by Emperor Wen who created a peaceful atmosphere by abolishing inhumane punishment, lightening the people's tax burden, and spending the rest of his modest life doing nothing in particular. As a result, peace and prosperity reigned, but under such conditions the powerful usually become more powerful and the weak tend to become weaker. Small wonder, then, that the feudal princes, noblemen, and powerful local families acquired large domains and large numbers of slaves and lived in luxury. In this ancient empire, the rich and powerful lived only with wine and sex in mind and completely disregarded morals.

Chao I, a scholar of the Ch'ing dynasty, points out that the life of feudal princes of the Han dynasty was utterly degenerate. Sons had children through their fathers' concubines and elder brothers stole the wives of their younger brothers and kept them as concubines. Siblings indulged in incest, while princes encouraged their favorite concubines to have intercourse with their favorite slaves. Some even stripped their court ladies and forced them to have intercourse with dogs and horses in disgusting attempts to produce a cross between man and beast. When asked why he indulged in such degrading acts, one of the princes confessed: "After losing my parents while I was still a child, I spent the rest of my life with eunuchs and court ladies. My chief retainer did not bother to teach me morals."

Such decadence was not so much the product of moral corruption as the reflection of a society where morals were practically unknown. In the early days of the Han dynasty, traces of the harshness of war remained and society in general was lacking in etiquette and refinement. Vendettas were considered praiseworthy, and swaggering gallants were much in evidence. Feudalism was predominant; soldiers were brave and strong. The well-armed Han soldier, it is said, was as good as six soldiers of the northern tribes, definitely not the case in the T'ang and Sung dynasties.

At this time of unbridled lawlessness Emperor Wu appeared on the scene. This heroic ruler was widely known for his great military campaigns, extravagant parties, prodigality, mercurial temper, arrogance, and wisdom. But only three points will be discussed here.

Emperor Wu officially sanctioned Confucianism. This was one of the most significant events in the history of China, which in the Earlier and Later Han dynasties alone not only brought about the widespread propagation of Confucianism, but also was largely responsible for bringing the eunuchs and Confucianists into direct opposition.

Confucianism was first employed during the reign of the first Han Emperor, with an eye to introducing etiquette into the Imperial court. Since the ministers and generals of the time were rough warriors of humble origin, their behavior at court banquets was hardly in keeping with etiquette. Intoxicated, they would boast of their achievements, quarrel, shout with drunken abandon, and end up slashing the nearest pillar with their swords.

These embarrassing scenes caused the Emperor great annoyance. Shu Sun T'ung, a onetime Confucianist, offered to bring the rowdy lot under control. He summoned thirty Confucianists from Shantung Province, the cradle of Confucianism, and asked them to lecture on etiquette. Some, however, refused on the ground that Shu Sun T'ung was a sycophant who curried favor with the powerful. Nevertheless, the ceremony held the following year for the completion of a new palace building proceeded in order, without even a cough from the solemn participants. Impressed, the Emperor commented proudly: "Now I know what a great honor it is to be a ruler." As a reward, Shu Sun T'ung was put in charge of court ceremonies. Actually, however, the ceremony had proceeded smoothly since a specially appointed officer promptly arrested those who refused to obey orders.

Thus Confucianism helped to make the leaders gentlemen and to establish a well-organized hierarchy around the ruler.

Emperor Wu had Confucianism included in the curriculum of the highest academic institution. Such works of Confucius as *Shih Ch'ing,* a collection of poems sung to the accompaniment of classical music, *Shu Ching,* an anthology of Imperial edicts, and *Ch'un Ch'ou,* a study of history, were officially adopted for education. The people of the Han dynasty regarded these tomes in much the same way as present-day Europeans regard Greek and Latin classics. They took to Confucianism with such enthusiasm that it eventually formed the basis of their political structure.

Wu unwittingly consolidated the position of the Empress' relatives. This began when he appointed Wei Ch'ing, Empress Wei's younger brother, to a military post. The Emperor ordered

138

this onetime bodyguard of one of his daughters to lead his army against the Huns (Hsung Nu). His victory was so impressive that he was not only made a peer and granted a fief, but was promoted to the highest military rank of Grand Marshal.

The Emperor had such faith in him that he even called him to the lavatory. One Chinese scholar points out that this shows that the Emperor looked down on his minister with contempt, while another claims it indicates that the Emperor was extremely fond of the Grand Marshal. The Imperial lavatory, unlike the odoriferous counterpart of the masses, was an elaborate setup with silk draperies, a magnificent bed, and two court ladies in attendance holding bags of incense.

The Imperial lavatory, actually, was the scene of many important decisions in the Han dynasty. Emperor Wu reportedly first became acquainted with Empress Wei there, and it was also in the lavatory that Emperor Huan of the Later Han dynasty worked out plans with his trusted eunuchs to eliminate his maternal relatives. Wei

Ch'ing stood high in the Emperor's favor, and all three of his sons were raised to the peerage. Further, his nephew was a great general; thus the Wei family became noblemen of the highest order.

Emperor Wu was also notorious for meting out punishment. It is reported that the Chao Yu, a prison whose inmates were confined by Imperial order, held as many as 70,000 prisoners. The premier of the time reasoned with the monarch that although he went to great trouble to acquire able subjects, he would soon run out of such men if he continued to imprison or execute them before they were given a chance to show their worth. Many famous and capable men were castrated as punishment. As a result, the quality of eunuchs, who were generally considered symbols of ignorance, improved to a degree never again attained in Chinese history.

Such a system obviously would eventually bring about the participation of the eunuchs in state affairs and mold them into powerful cliques since they were closest to the throne.

Eunuch's Daughter Becomes Empress

It was no easy task to straighten out the situation after the death of the powerful, absolute ruler Emperor Wu. Emperor Shao, for whom Emperor Wu had had great hopes, died without an heir at the age of twenty. Prince Ch'ang I, Lady Li's son, succeeded Chao to the throne, but was soon dethroned because of unseemly conduct. The next ruler was Emperor Hsuan, a ruler of strange destiny. The thorny issue of succession had been created by Emperor Wu himself. Hastily concluding that Crown Prince Wei had revolted, the short-tempered autocrat had had the Crown Prince, his three sons and daughter, and all of his concubines executed without so much as an investigation. Empress Wei, too, was forced to commit suicide.

Only the infant grandson of the Crown Prince, then several months old, survived the bloodbath. The infant prince, named Ping I, was so-called because he was weak. He was confined in a remote prison, for the central prison was filled with those accused of complicity in the incident.

Ping Chi, the deputy minister of law, who later became a premier, put the prince in an airy cell and ordered a female inmate to take care of him.

On hearing from a soothsayer, however, that there were signs indicating that the prison held a future ruler, Emperor Wu ordered the execution of all inmates. When the eunuch bearing the Imperial order arrived, however, Ping Chi closed the prison gates and refused to let him in. He was about to be accused of insubordination, but Emperor Wu changed his mind and called off the executions.

Chang He, who had at first been given the death sentence for serving Crown Prince Wei but whose sentence was later commuted to castration, was in charge of the Imperial harem. The faithful eunuch took pity on the young prince and paid for his education out of his own pocket.

When the young prince reached manhood, Chang He thought of having him marry his daughter, but was advised against it by his younger brother. He then tried to have the prince marry the daughter of eunuch Hsu Kuang Han, his subordinate, who had been castrated at the order of Emperor Wu (who at first ordered him to be executed merely because he had put the wrong saddle on the monarch's mount). "If your daughter marries the prince," he told Kuang Han, "you will at least be made a peer, since the prince is closely related to Emperor Chao." The two were united in wedlock. Thus the prince became an emperor—Emperor Hsuan. His wife Empress Hsu, the daughter of eunuch Kuang Han, gave birth to a son who became Emperor Yuan.

Affecting the ways of a dandy, Emperor Hsuan was fond of cockfights and horse races, but at the same time he was a wise, erudite ruler. He extended the terms of competent local officials to give ample scope to their administrative ability. As a result, more and more people supported the Han dynasty. His wisdom and popularity can be largely attributed to the fact that, until the age of eighteen, he lived among the people in a highly competitive world.

Since Emperor Hsuan was related to a eunuch, it could be assumed that the eunuchs would some day form a clique close to the throne—which is actually what happened. After twenty years of honest administration on behalf of the crown, Kuang offered to return the reins of government to the ruler since he had succeeded, despite dangerous odds, in seating Emperor Hsuan on the throne. It is often difficult to withdraw at the right moment; Kuang was no exception. His daughter was then Emperor Hsuan's consort, as the result of an evil plot contrived by her mother. Lady Hsien, a vain woman, wanted above all to seat her daughter on the throne, next to the Emperor. But the coveted position was occupied by a eunuch's daughter. Motivated by jealousy, she had pregnant Empress Hsu poisoned by one of the Empress' female physicians. Thus she succeeded in making her daughter Empress.

It was soon announced, however, that the grandchild of a eunuch would be made Crown Prince. This was too much for the evil woman, who ordered the Empress, her daughter, to poison the Crown Prince. But his nurse became suspicious and guarded him carefully. Upon learning of these diabolic acts, Kuang died in despair, and the Huo family, its mainstay gone, soon lost all power and glory. All members of this once illustrious family were executed as the result of the poisoning report and the plot for power. The Empress also was removed from the throne.

With the downfall of this powerful clique, Emperor Hsuan not only adopted a political policy based on a stringent penal system, but also appointed eunuchs to office, since they had neither relatives nor other undesirable ties. He also reinstated the secretarial system established by Emperor Wu, and put the eunuchs in charge of such duties as the appointment of officials and the handling of decisions on the memorials submitted to the throne. The Emperor had an ample staff of capable eunuchs since he had meted out punishment indiscriminately in the form of castration. Such eunuchs as Hung Kung, an authority on legislation, and Shih Hsien, a brilliant administrator, were of great help to the ruler. Officials with Confucian educations drew the Emperor's attention to the faults of such a system, but he refused to pay heed.

The gentle-hearted Crown Prince, a Confucianist at heart, urged his father to appoint more

Confucianists to office, since he decried the harsh penal policy enforced by the ruler. But the indignant Emperor answered: "The Han family has laws of its own. We resort to both government by power and government by morality. Confucianists as a rule are completely ignorant of the trend of the times. They only produce dreamers by praising the past and deriding the present. How can I possibly let such men hold the reins of government?" It must have been a great shock to the Emperor to learn that his son, the heir to the throne, was a follower of Confucianists.

Eunuchs Band Together

The day dreams that possessed Emperor Yuan, the son of Emperor Hsuan, were chiefly of Confucianism. But how was Confucianism, a common political ideology, transformed into the mysticism that was to so influence the Chinese rulers?

To answer this question, we must return to the time of Huo Kuang, when he was masterminding a *coup d'état*. Hsia Hou Sheng, the greatest Con-

fucianist of the age, had advised Prince Ch'ang
I Wang, the regent at that time, that he should
act with discretion because his antagonists were
plotting his downfall. Fearing that his plot had
been discovered, Huo Kuang visited Hsia Hou
Sheng and asked how he knew about his plans.
After reading a passage from the *Shu Ching,*
Sheng explained that he was able to make such a
prediction by comparing the present political
situation with the passage he had just quoted.
Kuang, an ex-soldier, and the ignorant leaders of
the government were so impressed with Sheng's
prescience that their respect for the Confucianists
was greatly enhanced. They appointed Sheng as
instructor to the Empress Dowager so that she
would, in time, be able to act as regent. Thus
Confucianism, which at first had been only a
means of teaching the rudiments of etiquette,
came to be regarded in the Imperial court as a
mystical system of prophecy. Clairvoyance capti-
vates people, regardless of time or place. Emperor
Yuan invited a large number of Confucianists to
court, listened to their lectures, and made them
government leaders.

The political situation changed. Capable Hung Kung and Shih Hsien served actively in politics as secretaries. Emperor Yuan left most of his affairs to them, believing that, since they were eunuchs, they would hardly join forces with external cliques. But trusted men often turn out to be villains. Hung Kung and his colleagues assumed absolute power, while the young ruler, ignorant of the ways of the world, was lost, as in a fever, in Confucianism. And the eunuchs increased their power by organizing themselves. As a result, state affairs came to be monopolized by eunuch ministers, whose power caused great concern in officialdom.

On the other hand, maternal relatives were automatically elevated to the peerage, made military commanders, and allowed free access to the Imperial court, in accordance with the unofficial system adopted in Huo Kuang's time. It is interesting to note that the two powerful and dangerous cliques were brought together by none other than the Confucianist officials, who were champions of justice.

Fully convinced that the two cliques were the

only obstacles to the emergence of a government under a sacred ruler, as expounded in the Confucianist doctrine, these officials criticized them with almost fanatic persistence. They called for the removal of onetime criminal eunuchs from their positions as secretaries, and they declared that it was ridiculous to grant a retainer special privileges simply because he happened to be the father of an Empress. In the face of such attacks, the maternal relatives had no choice but to join forces with the eunuchs. Since the Confucianists often cited divination, the eunuchs and their allies cast the more influential among them into prison.

Emperor Ch'eng, Yuan's successor, made changes. Not only did he remove Shih Hsien from power, but he relieved the eunuch secretaries of their duties, for he did not want the eunuchs to have exclusive powers. As a result, the once powerful eunuchs were relegated to the background.

But now the Confucianists were cooperating with the maternal relatives. The trend of the times was such that mystical Confucianism, by the force of its magic, might well have transformed everyone in the Imperial court into a dreamer. In such a court, only the person who had the qualifications of a sacred ruler would become Emperor. This fantastic dream was rendered into reality by Wang Mang, one of the maternal relatives, who had the makings of a saintly man.

Wang Mang, the son of Empress Dowager Wang's younger brother, studied Confucianism while impoverished. Wang gradually worked his way up to an influential post. He was greatly respected among the intellectuals, for he gave away the greater part of his fortune, while he himself lived modestly. About this time a strange prophecy, called the Ch'en Wei theory and expounded by the Ying Yang school of mysticism, prevailed. Taking full advantage of the prophecy, Wang Mang claimed that the time had come for a saint to replace the waning Han rulers —and that he was that saint.

To lend authenticity to his claim, Wang Mang resorted to subterfuge, declaring that stones bearing inscriptions to the effect that he was to be made Emperor rained down from Heaven. He had reports sent to the Emperor from all parts of the country to the effect that auspicious signs and prophecies in his favor had been witnessed. He also spread rumors that 30,000 poems praising his virtues and achievements had been sent to him from all parts of the country. Thus setting the stage for a forced abdication, Wang Mang did away with the Han dynasty and assumed the Imperial Throne.

Emperors and Ministers

The Han dynasty, brought into abeyance by Wang Mang's usurpation, was restored fifteen years later at the hands of the Liu brothers, aristocrats from the southern part of Honan Province who were distant relatives of the former Han rulers. The elder brother, Wu, died, and the younger brother, Wen, ascended the throne to become Emperor Kuang Wu, the first ruler of the Later Han dynasty.

Emperor Kuang Wu was well educated. As a youth he had studied Confucianism in the capital of Ch'ang An, but he was also a realist, for he had been in charge of manors. Kuang Wu took steps to prevent the emergence of cliques, he severed all ties between the eunuchs and the premier's office, since in the former dynasty the eunuchs had come to power as the result of such ties.

Now that the eunuchs were outcasts, the reform only served to bring the isolated eunuchs closer together. By commuting the death sentences given to notorious criminals, including those accused of high treason, to castration, the ruler increased the number of eunuchs. By his leniency, he enhanced the eunuchs' power.

Chapter VI

Eunuchs and Calamities Involving Women: T'ang Dynasty

Ch'ang An: Capital of Beauty and Immorality

In the T'ang dynasty, as in the Han and Ming dynasties, the eunuchs dominated the scene—but with a difference. Of the nine emperors who reigned during the last 100 years of the dynasty, seven were put on their thrones by eunuchs and the remaining two killed by them. This can only be taken as a reflection of the trends of the time.

Taoism, a folk religion peculiar to the Chinese; Buddhism; Manichaeism, a form of fire worship, and Nestorian Christianity, were practiced in this age. Religion then was in full bloom. Buddhism claimed the largest number of believers, followed

153

by Taoism, and the greater part of the population embraced one or the other.

Although both religions were originally ascetic in nature, in the hands of the people of the T'ang dynasty, they became means to satisfy human desires. This is eloquently described in a memorial submitted to the first Emperor of the dynasty, which called for the prohibition of Buddhism: "Buddhists confess their sins in the hope of gaining happiness in the future, give large sums of money to the poor in the hope of receiving extravagant rewards, and offer priests meals for a day in the hope of obtaining for themselves food for a hundred days. And when they are imprisoned, they pray to the Buddha for their release. Thus they claim that life and death, long life and short life, crime and punishment, happiness and virtue, riches and nobility, poverty and lowliness are all in the hands of the Buddha."

This shows that Buddhism, for the masses of the time, was a worldly religion. They were not concerned with what might happen to them after death; life for them was an endless series of earthly pleasures. Sins were forgotten and the people

154

lived for the fulfillment of their desires, for the
Buddha always protected them. So the people of
T'ang indulged in worldly pleasures with reli-
gious fervor.

If the Middle Ages could be called an age of
religion, so also could the T'ang dynasty, the
chief difference being that the Europeans rejected
heresies and were ascetics, if only in doctrinal
terms, whereas the Chinese of the T'ang accepted
the coexistence of a number of religions and were
hedonists.

In the T'ang dynasty, Confucianism played a
role similar to that played by ascetic nationalism
in Japan. Although Confucianism served as the
spiritual foundation of the Han Empire, it lost
considerable ground toward the end of Later Han.
This was largely because the people came to lose
faith in it. Contrary to its original nature, it had
grown into a doctrine that demanded of its followers illogical or even hypocritical acts. Confucianism then set great store by filial piety.
Obedient children were expected to observe
certain rites when a parent died. A son was
expected to set up a shack near his parent's grave

and live there for three years, wearing only crude hempen clothing. He was not only expected to avoid eating meal, but was forbidden to have sexual relations.

Naturally, a doctrine that called for such asceticism invited opposition and reaction. Small wonder, then, that in the Wei and Chin dynasties the nihilistic philosophy of Lao Tze and Lao Chuang acquired wide popularity.

But man cannot find real relief in nihilism. Buddhism had found its way into China from Central Asia. And it appealed to the people, since it taught that this world was only illusion and that peace could only be found on the "other shore." Temples and images were built as symbols of the world to come. Murals of brilliant hue and gold images of nude female deities served to create a world of fantasy. Thus an air of exoticism pervaded the temples, and the senses responded. Outside was the workday world, but it was nothing but an illusion. Was there, then, such a thing as an objective criterion by which good and evil could be distinguished? Only one's senses, one's desires were real. Wu San Ssu, Empress

Tsu T'ien Wu's nephew, gave eloquent expression to this attitude: "I don't know what people mean when they call one man good, and another evil. But as far as I am concerned, those who are good to me are good, and those who are not are evil."

Thus we see that in the T'ang dynasty the social setup was in sharp contrast to the strict Confucian society of the Later Han dynasty. The T'ang dynasty was a world empire, consisting of such races as the Chinese, Mongols, Turks, Tungus, and white Iranians. Unlike the Han and Sung dynasties, it was not exclusively Chinese. A culture of universal nature took root, while exclusive and nationalistic Confucianism waned. Ch'ang An, the largest city in the world at that time, was the center of this cosmopolitan culture. Here, apparel, music, and singing girls showed the influence of imported cultures, and since almost every race was represented, the inhabitants indulged in aesthetic and sensual pleasures, indifferent to such ideas as nationalism and patriotism. Under such conditions the pen flourished while the sword rusted.

Agents of Autocratic Emperors

The Ming was the last Chinese dynasty in which eunuchs wielded power. China underwent vast changes after the tenth century; with the elimination of the privileged nobility of T'ang, the rulers were brought into direct contact with the people. No longer under the control of the nobility, the emperors became stronger.

In the Han and T'ang dynasties absolute rule had prevailed and the officials had possessed power. But from the tenth century on, the foundation on which the bureaucratic system rested was different from that of the Han and T'ang dynasties.

In the Han dynasty, officials were appointed by recommendation, mostly by powerful clans. The appointment of lesser officials was left in the hands of the county and provincial governors. In the T'ang dynasty, on the other hand, the examination system had been adopted for the first time.

In the Sung dynasty, the situation changed. Poetry and literature, which had been the main subjects for examination candidates in T'ang, were replaced by ancient classics and political subjects. Furthermore, the final test was conducted by the Emperor himself.

Relations between the Chinese and alien races also underwent a major change in and after the tenth century. Following the downfall of the T'ang, many alien races—chiefly those in the north—invaded China by way of the Great Wall. Finally, the Mongols led by Kublai Khan overrode the land, transforming the Honan region—the center of culture and commerce that stretched south from the Yangtze basin—into a colony. They formed the Yuan dynasty. Under such conditions the Ming dynasty also was founded.

Abortive Attempt to Control Eunuchs

Fully aware that eunuchs had been powerful in T'ang, the first Ming Emperor did his best to keep them under control. At first, the eunuchs barely numbered 100, but toward the end of his reign, the number had increased considerably. As a result, the Emperor adopted a system calling for the establishment of twelve offices exclusively for eunuchs. And, in order to keep them under control, he not only forbade them to hold external offices, but limited the highest rank a eunuch could hold to the fourth official grade, or a grade below the deputy ministers of the external ministries. He had, coincidentally, adopted the system applied to the eunuchs of the T'ang dynasty. Furthermore, in order to sever the ties between eunuchs and officials, he prohibited the exchange of documents between the eunuchs' offices and the external offices. He even attached to the palace gate in the Inner Court a plaque bearing an inscription stating that any eunuch who meddled in politics would be executed. But even these stern measures failed.

Last of the Eunuchs

I have tried to shed light on the position of the eunuchs who formed an indispensable part of the Chinese system of absolute rule. Although it was in the Ming dynasty that they took full advantage of their unique position, the eunuch system in the Ch'ing dynasty must also be dealt with briefly, for it was the last dynasty of the empire.

As is generally know, the Ch'ing dynasty was founded by a conquering Manchurian tribe related to the Tungus. After establishing Peking as their capital and unifying China under their rule, the way of life of the Manchus changed considerably. During the reign of the first and second emperors in Manchuria, for instance, there was no eunuch system in use. Only after Emperor Shun Chih entered China proper and borrowed most of the Ming systems was the use of eunuchs adopted. Even then, the number of eunuchs was small in comparison with that of the Ming dynasty. According to an Imperial mandate issued by Emperor K'ang Hsi in 1710, there were only 400 or 500 eunuchs, as against 100,000 in Ming. Later, the number increased even more. In the T'ung Chih and the Kuang Hsu eras (the latter half of the nineteenth century), there were about 2,000 eunuchs in all, according to Stent.

In the Ch'ing dynasty, the offices and duties of eunuchs were much the same as in the Ming, with a few exceptions. In Ch'ing, the eunuchs were forbidden to leave the capital. Also, whereas only the emperors could keep eunuchs in Ming, members of the Imperial family were allowed this privilege in Ch'ing. The lesser members kept about four eunuchs, while those of higher rank employed as many as thirty. Presumably, the Imperial family kept eunuchs as substitutes for slaves, for it had been customary for them to keep slaves in Manchuria.

Until the days of Empress Dowager Hsi, well toward the end of the dynasty, there were scarcely any major incidents caused by eunuchs, not only because they were few in number but also because the rulers—notably Emperors K'ang Hsi, Yung Cheng, and Ch'ien Lung—ruled wisely. The chief exception was the rebellion of the believers in T'ien Li Chao during the reign of Emperor Jen Tsung, in 1813.

The T'ien Li Chao was a sect of the Pai Lien Chiao, a secret religious organization, whose credo was that through Maitreya, the Buddha of the Future, the world would undergo complete reform. This revolutionary religion had many

162

followers among the masses. They revolted in the first year of Emperor Jen Tsung's reign and caused great confusion in north and central China for the ensuing ten years. Some time after the rebellion had been quelled, the followers of T'ien Li Chao rose in arms in Hua, in the northern part of Honan, and in Peking. In Peking, seventy T'ien Li Chao rebels, disguised as peasants and guided by seven eunuchs, scaled the Tung Hua and Hsi Hua gates to storm the Palace.

Most of the eunuchs of the time were from a district in Hopei where the T'ien Li Chao flourished. It seems that the followers had spread the religion among them, and that the eunuchs sided with them in the uprising. This incident, then, could hardly be called an evil caused by the eunuchs themselves.

The evil influence of the Ch'ing eunuchs was first felt in the days of the Empress Dowager Hsi, who came from the Manchu nobility. Since Emperor T'ung Chih, Emperor Hsien Feng's successor, was then only five years old, Empress Dowager Tung, the late Emperor Hsien Feng's wife, and Empress Dowager Hsi, Emperor T'ung

Chih's real mother, acted as his regents with the help of Prince Kung, the Emperor's uncle. This form of government closely resembled that of the relatives on the maternal side during the Han dynasty.

Singularly resourceful, Empress Dowager Hsi dominated the scene. She also favored eunuchs. An Te Hai was the first eunuch who found favor with her. Born of poor parents who forced castration on him at the age of twelve, he was quite handsome in 1855. Empress Dowager Hsi, who loved him like a son, chose him, and when she became regent he participated in the government.

The next eunuch who found favor with Empress Dowager Hsi was Li Lien Ying. For forty years, from the end of the T'ung Chih era, he wielded tremendous power, with her support. A native of Hopei, the cradle of eunuchs, he was the son of a hooligan. A vagabond himself, Li was thrown into a local prison for selling contraband nitrate of soda. After regaining freedom he became a shoemaker, but since that got him nowhere he volunteered to be castrated on the advice of a eunuch friend from Hopei.

On learning that Empress Dowager Hsi wanted to have her hair done after the fashion then popular in Peking and that none of the eunuchs had been able to please her, Li Lien Ying visited a house of pleasure to learn the style. He then returned to the Palace and coiffured Empress Dowager Hsi's hair the way she wanted it. From that time on, he became her favorite.

By virtue of the Empress Dowager's authority, Li amassed a large fortune by accepting bribes. When the Boxer Rebellion erupted, he buried the money and fled to Sian with Emperor Kuang Hsu and the Empress Dowager. The money, however, was later confiscated.

The Boxer Rebellion was triggered by the I He T'uan, a secret organization affiliated with the Pai Lien Chiao religion. Advocating the protection of the Ch'ing Empire and the destruction of the Westerners, the rebels launched a powerful chauvinistic movement in the provinces of Shantung and Hopei by agitating among the poverty-stricken peasants and unemployed. Empress Dowager Hsi, herself a conservative and a chauvinist, secretly supported the movement, it was reported. Further, Prof. Hashikawa has pointed out that Li Lien Ying and a number of other eunuchs were connected with the rebels. Eunuchs from Hopei Province also had a hand in the T'ien Li Chao uprising; it is easy to conclude that eunuchs had much more to do with the rebellions toward the end of the Ch'ing dynasty than was once thought.

Another Ch'ing eunuch, an unusual character, should also be mentioned. By the name of K'ou Lien Ts'ai, he not only wrote a statement criticizing Empress Dowager Hsi's policies, but handed it to her personally. Among other things, he urged her to abolish the I He Yuan Wan Shou Shan Detached Palace, which she reportedly built with funds earmarked for a battleship; to relieve Li Hung Chang of his post because he was indecisive, and to step up armament in order to fight Japan. He also made the startling proposal that the next Emperor be chosen from the wise men of the empire, since Emperor Kuang Hsu was without heir. The statement enraged the Empress Dowager. At first, she thought there were others behind the plans, but on learning that K'ou Lien Ts'ai alone was responsible for the statement, she had him executed the year after the war with Japan ended (1896).

Thus the new age had penetrated the old world of the eunuchs. Modern trends were much in evidence throughout the empire; as a result, many intellectuals came to the conclusion that the eunuch system was anachronistic. Soon voices were raised for their abolition. Prof. Kuwabara said in 1923 : "It seems that the demand for complete abolition of eunuchs on the part of the Chinese began some twenty odd years ago, with Sun I Jang, the initiator, and his colleagues. If I remember correctly, Sun I Jang based his argument on the fact that the world powers did not have eunuchs, whereas eunuchs were kept by such weak countries as Turkey."

Presumably, Sun I Jang, who was an eminent Ch'ing archaeologist, made this statement immediately after the Boxer Rebellion. The fact that the complete abolition of the eunuchs was first demanded only after the advent of the twentieth century shows how deeply the eunuch system was rooted in Chinese history.

Empress Dowager Hsi, who was the last ruler in Chinese history to give full scope to the activities of eunuchs, died in 1908. In 1912, when the Ch'ing dynasty collapsed as a result of the republican revolution, the eunuch system died along with the autocracy that had supported it. By strange coincidence, the last eunuch of historical significance, Li Lien Ying, also died in 1912.

Appendix I

Why There Were No Eunuchs in Japan

Why were there no eunuchs in Japan? Many Japanese have probably asked themselves this question. I cannot answer with certainty, but I am able to theorize.

As I mentioned in the beginning of this book, the origin of the eunuch system is to be found in ancient societies. The *Wuo Jen Chuan,* a commentary on the Japanese found in the *Wei Chih,* an old Chinese history, is the oldest piece of historical literature on Japan. In this book the term Tung I, which means literally "eastern barbarians," seems to refer to a definite historical world. In the section of the *Ch'ien Han Shu* that deals with geography, there is a prophesy by Confucius that his teachings would one day be practiced in the land of Tung I.

In this case, Tung I refers to Manchuria, Korea,

and Japan, or in ethnical terms, to the Tungus, the Japanese, and the Koreans. As Confucius prophesied, apart from China, Confucianism was confined to these parts of the world. The people of the areas referred to had much in common. According to the *Wuo Jen Chuan,* the world of Tung I was one of hunting and farming communities based on the clan system. There were slaves, but no eunuchs.

As previously mentioned, castration was forbidden among peoples of the same blood; it can readily be seen why there were no eunuchs in the clan system. In Manchuria, the Ch'ing rulers were of a clan related to the Southern Tungus, but when they captured members of the more barbaric Northern Tungus tribes, they made them slaves but not eunuchs. It is presumed that they considered them brothers of a different culture and not aliens.

In the case of Japan, we know through ancient myths that in the Yamato age such alien tribes as the Izumo and Hayato formed one integral clan.

It follows that there existed neither the practice

of castration nor the use of eunuchs. Racially, they seem to have been the oldest of the Tung I group, and although no definite historical links have been established between the Yin race and the ancient Japanese, there were many points in common between the two as pointed out by Professors Konan Naito and Shizuka Shirakawa.

Why, then, were there eunuchs in the Yin dynasty and not in Japan? It will be recalled that the people of Yin had eunuchs only after they conquered the Ch'iang, a Tibetan tribe they considered alien. The subjugation of an alien race, it would seem, was an absolute requisite for the start of eunuchs. All eunuchs in the Turkish harems were either black or white—in other words, aliens.

In the ancient society of Japan there were no broad contacts with alien races. Nor did our ancestors conquer any alien races (contact with the southern half of the Korean Peninsula could hardly be considered contact with aliens). Therefore, one major reason why there were no eunuchs in Japan was because of its isolated position.

The Japanese at that time had adopted the

171

T'ang five-point penal system which consisted of flogging, caning, imprisonment, exile, and execution. Castration, however, was not included. Furthermore, since Buddhism flourished in Japan, there was no place for such a cruel form of punishment.

Appendix II

Eunuch-like Men in Modern Times

Can it be claimed that eunuchs are now only a nightmarish part of the past? This may sound ridiculous, but it bears consideration.

As Sun I Jang pointed out, both China and Turkey—lands of eunuchs—perished because of internal weakness at the turn of the century, and countries in which eunuchs were never known dominate today's world. Moreover, since humanism and rationalism have come to be the guiding principles of our age, the rebirth of a eunuch system is inconceivable.

Eunuch-like men, however, are still among us today. Returning briefly to the origin of eunuchs, it will be recalled that in the theocratic Yin dynasty, where the rulers were considered sacred, eunuchs were employed to preserve secrets. These eunuchs not only served as secretaries but formed cliques. The word "secretary" derives from the word "secret;" thus eunuchs may be called the first secretaries in history. When we compare the Ch'ing dynasty and the Turkish régimes, we find that they were theocracies—the Turkish sultans serving as protectors of the faith and the Ch'ing emperors, supported by Confucian precepts, serving as Heaven's deputies.

In these theocratic dynasties, the members of the cabinets served as the rulers' unofficial secretaries. As cliques, however, the eunuchs exercised greater authority than cabinet members because they were closer to the throne.

Since there was no place in the theocracies of China and Turkey for rationalism and humanism, the creation of eunuchs was a natural result. Based on this reasoning, there is no room for eunuchs in our modern world. Yet I cannot help feeling that the ghosts of eunuchs are still active today. If it is true that eunuchs were the product of power structures, then it should be equally true that people similar to the eunuchs exist today, for such power structures still exist, although altered in form.

Dehumanization by castration is out of the question today, but it seems that we, as men, are being stripped of our manhood in the sense that we are becoming only part of a system. We are woven into large organizational nets in one form or another in all areas of society. Large firms employ enough people to populate a town or a city, and they have organized them through "scientific management." As a result, such men now constitute only units or numbers in huge organizations.

It might be pointed out that in America, asexual tendencies have become a subject of concern. Dehumanization of the organizational man can no longer be dismissed as just a theory. Perhaps it can be said that we are fast becoming eunuchs in a psychological sense.

Many are inclined to believe that absolute rulers wielded tremendous power, but by present-day standards, their power was considerably limited. This is suggested by the remark of a subject under autocratic rule: "When the sun rises I till my land, and when it sets I rest. The emperor's power means nothing to me." In comparison, the power of today's great organizations is tremendous.

When we remember that the eunuchs functioned best in the T'ang dynasty, which had the best administrative organization in Chinese history, it can be seen that secretarial bodies do not clash with well-organized institutions. We can assume that organs directly attached to management will play increasingly important roles.

The question is whether modern secretarial groups can escape the stigma that was attached to eunuchs. One reason for arrogance on the part of eunuchs was their deep involvement in the private lives of the emperors. In this respect, it should be noted that the spirit of harmony has long served as the guiding principle in Japanese organizations, that enterprises are communities and government offices are large families. Those belonging to an organization, public or private, are expected to share one another's fortunes and misfortunes. And eunuch-like existences, in the form of groups directly attached to those in power, are by no means alien to our modern age.